GU00982957

Fighting Slavery –

Faith in Action

Nick Kinsella & Peter Stanley, + Audrey Stanley
Executive Editors

RIVER
PUBLISHING

River Publishing & Media Ltd
Barham Court
Teston
Maidstone
Kent
ME18 5BZ
United Kingdom

info@river-publishing.co.uk

ISBN 978-1-908393-45-6
Cover design by www.spiffingcovers.com
Printed in the United Kingdom

Contents

Acknowledgements   4

Introduction   5

1. Fighting Slavery: Faith in Action – James Ewins   7

2. Seeking Justice is Hard – John Cotton Richmond   17

3. iCampaign – Danny Smith   29

4. The Mission to End Slavery – Father Shay Cullen   41

5. Hiding in Plain Sight – Clint and Rebecca Dunning   53

6. Hope for Justice – Ben Cooley   65

7. A Change of Perspective – Peter Stanley   75

8. Let the Slaves Speak – Baroness Caroline Cox   91

9. Cargo – Paul Field   113

10. Twenty-seven Million – Beth Redman   123

11. Do You Want to Travel Fast? Or Do You Want
    to Travel Far? – Antonie Fountain   129

12. A Community against Trafficking – Peter Cox   137

13. The Salvation Army's Fight against Slavery – Anne Read 143

14. A Safe House for Survivors – Tina English   151

15. My Justice Journey – Danielle Strickland   167

16. Aware and Convinced, Compassionate and Collaborative –
    Bishop Pat Lynch   175

17. Trafficking in Human Persons – A Joined-up Response –
    Sister Imelda Poole   179

18. Crime Stoppers and Human Trafficking in the US – John Lamb 193

19. The US Catholic Bishops' Fight against Human Trafficking –
    Bishop Eusebio L. Elizondo   203

20. Fighting Slavery – the Irish Government's Response –
    Marion Walsh   215

21. Bringing the Law to Bear upon Modern Slavery –
    Baroness Elizabeth Butler-Sloss   231

22. Law Enforcement Can't Deal With This On Its Own –
    Nick Kinsella   237

Signs That a Person May be a Victim of Human Trafficking   251

Acknowledgements

My friend and fellow executive editor, Nick, and I have often chatted about the unsung heroes of the fight against slavery that we both admire. During car journeys together we spoke of priests and nuns around the world who were risking their lives to keep victims safe from traffickers; about the church minister who gave up his job to nightly risk his life investigating the brothels of Mumbai. There were many other gutsy individuals made mention of – people of faith living dangerous lives in order to protect or rescue others – unseen by the majority.

The world of human trafficking is dark, very dark, yet such brave people are lights, showing the way. They inspire me, but I draw more inspiration still from my faith and dedication to Jesus, who Himself risked everything to protect and rescue humanity. I dedicate this book to the next generation who I see have such a hunger for justice, and to my lawyer wife, Gillie, and our kids, Jo, Lizzie and Luke. My hope is that they too will gain further inspiration to fight for justice and sing the songs of freedom.

Peter Stanley, March 2015

Peter has captured above our motivation to publish this book and I share his dedication of this work to the future generation of abolitionists. I dedicate this book to my family: my wife, Mary, our children, Joe, Fran, Craig and Clare, and to our grandchildren – the youngest of whom, our beautiful Orlaith Bridie, who was born just three days ago.

Nick Kinsella, March 2015

Introduction

The personal stories of twenty-two people from various parts of the world are gathered here to inform readers about the battle taking place to counter the evil of modern day slavery. They prove that the motivation that comes from a Christian faith, which values human life, can achieve truly great things.

The contributors to this book have written chapters in their own style to illustrate the fight against slavery taking place in a wide range of contexts and cultures. We hear from a London barrister, a Dutch lobbyist, a Philippine priest, national and local safe house managers, bishops, the founder of the UK Human Trafficking Centre, a senior civil servant, a musical producer, US abolitionists, the president of Crime Stoppers USA, members of the UK House of Lords and Salvationists from the UK and Canada. Each one writes their story to encourage and challenge you to join them in *Fighting Slavery – Faith In Action*.

By purchasing this book you have taken the first step as we, the executive editors, will donate all profits from the sale of this book to victims and survivors of slavery. We are also delighted and grateful that the publishers have also committed to make their own contribution.

Peter Stanley, Executive Editor

Chapter 1
Fighting Slavery: Faith in Action
James Ewins

It was on 9 February 2007 that I first became aware of modern slavery, almost exactly 200 years after William Wilberforce succeeded in his campaign to abolish the transatlantic slave trade. I attended an event at St Paul's Church Hammersmith in West London, put on by Stop the Traffik.

When I look back now, I wonder why it has had such a profound effect on me – I've been to so many events, talks, and presentations in my life about pressing social issues. But none had the impact of that evening.

Perhaps I was particularly susceptible that night. I was recovering from a second bout of lymphoma for which I had been treated with high-dose chemotherapy and a stem cell transplant. This was one of the first times I had been out on my own in over a year, and I was beginning to appreciate, more acutely than ever before, that there might be a divine purpose in my survival. Regardless, on that evening my life radically changed direction.

I had been a Christian since the age of 16 and was actively involved in my local church. Happily married to my amazing wife,

Tiffany-Alice, with two wonderful children, I had a successful career as a barrister. I enjoyed marathon running, sailing and skiing.

But the experience of cancer had drawn me into the community of suffering from which I had been relatively immune thus far in my life. Perhaps the presentation tapped into that fresh awareness and connection I felt with vulnerability. It contained testimony from people engaged with human trafficking in the UK and abroad; it relayed distressing stories and facts; it presented songs – an entire musical, in fact – about human trafficking; and it ended with a call to action.

The speaker invited us to respond in one of several ways. First, there was a stall of handicrafts made by women who had been freed from sexual slavery in India, which we could buy to support their rehabilitation and awareness program.

Secondly, Compassion UK had a table with the details of hundreds of children who could be sponsored, giving them an education, healthcare and opportunities they could not have dreamed of. We would then be helping them avoid the traps that so often lead to slavery.

Third, Stop the Traffik were running a campaign to try and make more chocolate manufacturers use and produce fairly-traded cocoa – we could sign a petition and resolve to boycott non-Fairtrade chocolate.

Or finally, maybe, just maybe, someone would be willing to pick up the baton that William Wilberforce ran with for nearly all his life, and give their lives and energies to the fight against slavery.

I bought a small felt bag in the shape of a butterfly for £5. I took away the leaflets about child sponsorship. But the invitation to take up the cause that William Wilberforce gave his life for was ringing in my ears. When I got home that evening, Tiffany-Alice realized immediately that something dramatic had happened. And, as usual, she was right.

Over the following days and weeks I was consumed with the desire to respond to what I had heard. I was spurred on by learning that my house was located in what was formerly William Wilberforce's back garden, in south London! So, I looked into the work of Compassion UK and found out which of their projects were in areas where slavery was rife. I suggested to my church leaders at St Mark's Battersea Rise, that we aim to sponsor as many children in those locations as were in our own Sunday school.

In November 2007 we presented the work of Compassion UK to the church and over 100 children were sponsored that day. Since then, over 100 more have been sponsored. As a family we decided to give up our subscription to Sky television and instead sponsored a child for each of our, eventually four, children.

The next thing I did was to research the social policies of Cadbury, my favorite chocolate. One of Stop the Traffik's major campaigns was focused on the lives of children forced into slavery in the cocoa farms of West Africa.

Despite my near-obsessive penchant for Cadbury's Dairy Milk, I gathered together all the Cadbury chocolate products we had in our home, from cooking cocoa to drinking chocolate to Dairy Milk bars, and returned them all to Cadbury with a long letter explaining my resolve not to eat Cadbury chocolate again until they were taking adequate steps to ensure the fair treatment of workers, especially children, in their supply chains.

They replied by calculating the approximate value of all the chocolate I had returned and sending me a check for about £31. I cashed the check and thanked them for the founding donation for my campaign to turn them into a Fairtrade supplier.

Along with a friend from St Mark's Church, Matt Trendall, we began an ongoing dialogue with the Corporate Social Responsibility department of Cadbury UK. Over the course of two years and a number of meetings they initiated the Cadbury Cocoa Partnership. In 2009, they began to produce Fairtrade Dairy Milk, and I ate my first Cadbury chocolate in two years!

Meanwhile, a more profound change was taking place in me. In the summer of 2007, Scott Lewis, from an American charity called International Justice Mission (IJM), came to speak at St Mark's. He explained that IJM works for victims of violent injustice around the world. It operates on a casework model, by providing practical and legal support for individual victims, helping them to secure the protection to which they are entitled under the local law, bringing perpetrators to justice and then leveraging what they learn from their numerous cases to bring about transformation of the public justice system.

In order to do this work, IJM recruits investigators, lawyers and social workers. I distinctly remember the friends I was sitting with in church that morning nudging me as the obvious connection between my legal training and my passion to combat modern slavery was played out in the work of IJM. I went to a lunch gathering at which I, somewhat presumptuously, asked about working for the organization. More of that later.

In the meantime, I came to read a book called *Good News about Injustice* written by IJM's founder and CEO, Gary Haugen. It reminds me of the moment when my son and one of his best friends realized that they had something in common they had not known about before – in their case, a love of Star Wars. It was rather like that with me and God: I realized that we both loved justice. There were two particular parts of Gary's book that formed a foundation upon which everything I have done since then is built.

The first is the realization that justice is at the center of God's heart and that it is at the forefront of his agenda for the church and the world. We read in Micah 6:8 what the Lord requires of us: that we love mercy, do justice, and walk humbly with our God. In Matthew 23:23, Jesus rebukes the Pharisees for neglecting the more important matters of the law: justice, mercy and righteousness. So, in both the Old and New Testaments, where we are presented with God's three-point manifesto, justice is included.

The second is a story based on the feeding of the 5,000. Gary asks rhetorically what would have happened if, when Jesus performed the miracle of multiplying the bread and fish and asked the disciples to distribute it to the crowd, they had thanked him profusely, but had not got on with the job. What if they had spent their energy marveling at the miracle, but not actually delivering its benefits to those in need?

These two principles: the centrality of justice and the imperative of responding with action, left me in no doubt about what was required of me. I had the privilege of being brought up in a loving home, receiving a good state education, going to Oxford University, and becoming an expert in 'justice.' Now I realized how God felt about injustice, I was compelled to act. The only question was: How?

At the same time, Tiffany-Alice and I were taking part in a course at St Mark's Church called the 'Adventure of Living,' designed to help people consider how God may be calling them to do something radically different from their current work. It ends by channeling all of the learning, prayer and guidance included throughout the course into drafting a personal mission statement. It is fair to say that my personal mission statement was as much of a shock to me as it was to others, because at the center of it was a passion and declared intention to free slaves.

In the spring of 2008, Tiffany-Alice and I travelled to Washington, DC for IJM's annual conference, the Global Prayer Gathering. It was an opportunity to hear first-hand accounts of the work of IJM, to meet its staff from around the world and, above all, to pray for their work and the victims whom they serve. It was an utterly inspiring time. I have returned to the Global Prayer Gathering every year since then, and it remains as inspiring as it was in 2008 and a high point of my year. While at the Gathering I attended a prayer meeting led by Philip Langford, the Field Office Director of the Bangalore office. I was moved by the horror of bonded labor of which he spoke, but also struck by his humility and the fact that he, like me, was a qualified lawyer who had understood the importance of justice to God.

Philip had moved with his family from the comfort of the USA to serve God in India and I asked him if I could travel to see what it was like to serve overseas with IJM. He agreed, although he tells me now that he was skeptical that I would ever in fact go. However, in May 2008, I flew to Bangalore for five days, leaving Tiffany-Alice, who was by then six months pregnant, and our two other children at home.

I should pause to emphasize that these steps were not normal for me. Our life in England, despite my illness, was comfortable and safe. We were committed to our faith, very involved in our local church, and my success as a barrister enabled us to be relatively generous givers. But something else was at work here.

The call of God was not limited by my previous experience, desires, understanding, or perceived horizons. It acted like a force of galactic proportions pulling me out of the comfort of my regular orbit into an auto-rickshaw on the streets of Bangalore. Philip and his family graciously detailed the reality of living in India with a young family, answering the hundred of questions that Tiffany-Alice and I had prepared, and the IJM staff generously included me in their work. I returned knowing that this was not only a unique opportunity to offer the skills I had, but that it was doable and I could reasonably ask my family to support me. And so I wrote my CV (for the first time in 12 years) and sent it to IJM. They had no vacancies at that time, but said they would hold my CV on their file.

It was in October 2008 that I received a phone call. They had potential openings in Cambodia and in Bangalore (Philip was being promoted). So I flew out to Washington DC for interviews and informed my referees to expect a call. I was asked to attend a final interview with Sean Litton, the Vice President of Field Operations, who would be passing through the UK in November 2008.

It transpired that Sean and I would be attending the same event in Birmingham. 'The Stand' was the inaugural event of the Hope for

Justice charity, organized by my great friend Ben Cooley, who like me had been inspired by the Stop the Traffik events of 2007. After speaking to the thousands of people there about my journey of justice so far, I went off to a side room to be interviewed by Sean. His questions came to a crescendo with this: 'Are you prepared to die doing this?' Sean pulled no punches and, as I was later to find out, he was right to do so.

About two weeks later, as I was giving a talk in the House of Lords on behalf of IJM, I received the momentous email offering me the role of Field Office Director in Bangalore. Then followed several very busy weeks in which I had to wrap up my legal practice, undergo essential training and Tiffany-Alice and I had to prepare to move continent.

The time that I spent serving through IJM in Bangalore was indescribably amazing. As the Field Office Director I had responsibility not only for our casework performance, but also for the care of the team. I was leading our morning prayer meetings, mentoring our team of lawyers with immensely challenging legal problems, overseeing the investigation and after-care work in the office and the administrative support. Most importantly, however, the focus of my role was to invest in the national staff: 96% of IJM's staff are local to their now 18 field offices.

On some days, we would strategize about how to penetrate a brick kiln or rock quarry to gain the trust of slaves to tell their story for a case against the perpetrators. On other days we would prepare arguments for the various legal proceedings running concurrently. On some days we would wait in government offices for a meeting with an official who was deliberately avoiding us, not wanting to face up to the reality of slavery within his jurisdiction. And on other days, we would accompany the police to rescue whole families who had been enslaved and had lived in daily fear of their lives for months, years or generations.

The work could be dangerous, as owners did not take kindly to their slaves being freed. They were quick to rouse mobs to act in their defense, often frightening the police into retreat and leaving us at risk of being attacked. More than once, we left a scene at high speed, while rocks were thrown at our vehicle. But we never gave up; we would always come back. It is a testimony to my colleagues' bravery and tenacity, expressing a characteristic of our heavenly Father: I will never leave you or forsake you.

Tiffany-Alice would take up residence on the terrace on our roof and pray for my safe return and for the success of our mission. It was exhilarating, exhausting, challenging and rewarding. But it all came to a painfully premature end when I had to return to the UK as the lymphoma had returned after I had been in Bangalore less than two years.

I had no time to say goodbye to my staff (I found a lump in my neck on a Sunday afternoon, and flew home to the UK for a check-up on Monday morning), leaving Tiffany-Alice, who was by then six months pregnant with our fourth child, to arrange the return of the family and our belongings to the UK, where I had started chemotherapy. Our church stepped in and helped find a home for the family to arrive back in and places for the children in the local school.

After that traumatic return it took months to recover, even after chemotherapy had kicked the lymphoma into complete remission. But, as the stormy waves began to calm, and as we dared to look over the sides of our metaphorical boat again, the next opportunity to seek justice was soon upon me.

I decided to return to my career as a self-employed barrister, which gave me the autonomy to do what God had planned next. The renowned think tank, the Centre for Social Justice, was putting together a working committee to study slavery in the UK. A small group of friends had heard Gary Haugen talk about modern slavery and decided that the first step towards 21st century abolition was a proper understanding of the problem. They raised the funding for a 20-month study and published a report: 'It Happens Here: Equipping the United Kingdom to Fight Modern Slavery' in March 2013.

I was delighted to bring the understanding that I had gained, principally through IJM, to a UK context and to contribute to the report. I was also privileged to work with and meet many amazing abolitionists, committed to combatting modern slavery, many of whom had been doing so for far longer than me. I remain deeply inspired and hugely indebted to them for providing examples of best practice and innovation.

After publication of the report, we met with politicians, including the Cabinet Social Justice Committee, lobbying shamelessly for implementation of the report's findings. This was completely unchartered territory for me, but I was heartened by the responses we received, and delighted as more people joined the growing team of 21st century abolitionists.

Finally, a copy of the report found its way to the desk of the Home Secretary, Theresa May. In the summer of 2013 she decided to take up the cause and stated her intention to put a Modern Slavery Bill before Parliament before the general election in 2015. To this end, she commissioned an independent evidence review, chaired by Frank Field MP, which I was invited to join. On the same day that the report was published, 16 December 2013, the Home Office published a Draft Modern Slavery Bill.

In January 2014, a Joint Select Committee of the House of Commons and the House of Lords was established to conduct pre-legislative scrutiny of that Bill and I was asked to be a Special Advisor. That role will shortly be coming to a conclusion, as the committee reports to parliament. As this book goes to press, the Bill is completing its passage through the Lords, and it is hoped to pass successfully into law before the end of the current parliament in March 2015.

And so the journey continues. I do not know what God has next for me to do. All I can say is that I intend to pursue my calling to fight slavery with all I have, for as long as I can.

James Ewins is a barrister. He is married with four children. Since 2007, he has been engaged in fighting for the abolition of slavery both in the UK and abroad. He has worked as the Director of International Justice Mission's Bangalore office, and been involved in the research and drafting of the Modern Slavery Bill.

Chapter 2
Seeking Justice is Hard
John Cotton Richmond

Something is missing from the discussion about human trafficking. The typical presentation on this issue has three phases. It starts with an argument that the offence exists, often using a compelling story about a sympathetic victim. It then shifts to a strategy to engage the problem through law enforcement, victim care, or prevention. It concludes with a call to action through awareness, prayer, giving and participation.

These are good, necessary elements of the movement to combat the massive problem of slavery in our world today. Yet, there is an unspoken reality about seeking justice.

Seeking justice can be a hard, painful and slow endeavor. Setbacks, failure and sacrifice are common companions on the journey. Those engaged in the fight against modern slavery must know not only the importance of the cause, but also that combating it requires determination and perseverance. Justice comes through thoughtful, intense effort over time.

This perseverance is important because exploited people cannot be rescued through a well-intentioned spasm of activity. Justice demands the steady application of love in action that outlasts a trafficker's scheme. Traffickers often rely on an erratic pattern of enthusiasm in the world of philanthropy and international aid. If they can outlast the grant given to an NGO, or a governmental leader's term of service, they win. And the stakes could not be higher: the freedom of millions hangs in the balance.

At its essence, justice is making wrong things right. It is a fairly simple concept, but it is rarely easy. The fact that traffickers trap and exploit people is wrong. Holding them legally accountable and assisting victims as they return to a life of freedom, rights the wrong. This work may not erase the painful scars the traffickers inflicted, but it gives survivors the chance of recovery and restoration. Justice stops exploitation and generates hope for the future.

The men and women I have met around the world who seek justice for others are heroes. They do not wear capes and they do not possess superpowers. If you saw them on the street they would blend into their surroundings. Yet they have embraced the difficult work of righting wrongs, enduring personal hardship, pain and sacrifice to do so. I am fortunate to call many of these heroes my friends.

During my years in India leading International Justice Mission's anti-slavery work and my time prosecuting forced labor and sex trafficking cases in the United States, one thing has been constant. There are no easy human trafficking cases, and the difficulty of seeking justice can cause us to give up too soon. But for those who persevere, great joy and deep meaning can be found along this challenging path.

Of course, the importance of abolition ought to overshadow any discouragement and difficulty that accompanies it. But to have a sustained impact, with boots on the ground day in and day out, justice seekers must intentionally set aside time to prepare their minds for action.

Improbable hope

One day while living in India, I met several slaves who had escaped from a brick kiln. They described the harrowing details of their escape and the brutal conditions that led them to run away and risk everything. The workers in the kiln worked day and night for meager provisions, and were not allowed to leave. The situation had become so dire that they commissioned a few of their own to escape and find someone who could help. They were armed with nothing except an improbable hope.

Their situation, although illegal under Indian law, was culturally accepted and had become the status quo for the community. They had never heard of other similarly situated slaves being rescued. There was nothing in their experience to suggest that freedom was a possibility. Yet the cruel, dehumanizing circumstances of slavery drove a small group of them to flee their shanty homes within the kiln. They were not even sure that what they were searching for actually existed.

When we heard how the kiln owners recruited and trapped their victims, we were motivated to act. Our team of investigators, social workers, and lawyers began gathering sufficient evidence for the government to apply the protections of Indian law. My colleagues had a passion for righting wrongs and were committed to walk this difficult path toward justice with the victims, but neither group knew what the next few months would require of them.

The core difficulty

Human trafficking cases are difficult for many reasons. The victims often have troubled and problematic lives. Some have criminal records or have illegally crossed borders. Many have suffered abuse at the hands of others before being targeted by their trafficker. For a variety of reasons, many victims are reluctant to trust the authorities and cooperate when help finally arrives.

Heaped upon the personal challenges confronting a victim are broader issues of lack of clean water, sustainable food supply, education, medical care, reliable government actors, and economic opportunity. These problems can create a toxic cocktail of vulnerability. Traffickers seek victims already tangled up in difficult circumstances because they are often easier to exploit.

Yet all these problems are not the core difficulty in combating human trafficking. They merely generate the vulnerability that traffickers exploit. Towering above all these significant challenges in human trafficking cases is the trafficker's willful decision to profit by harming others.

When we seek to aid people dealing with prolonged drought, we are working against the natural elements. Water does not willfully refuse to fall from the sky or try to conceal the effects of thirst or crop failure to prevent people of good will from helping. People can affect or exacerbate environmental problems, but the drought itself was not caused by human decision.

When we seek to help ill people, we are working against disease. Viruses and bacteria do not plot and scheme about people they might target. They do not engage in fraud or set traps to render certain people sick. The illness is not choosing to harm people for its own financial benefit or willfully obstructing medical professionals from providing care.

But when we seek justice, we work against a human adversary. There is a trafficker scheming to exploit the vulnerable and conceal the crime. Oppressors deliberately work against the justice we seek. Making wrong things right is made exceptionally difficult because others are scheming to profit by making right things wrong.

The adversary

As my heroic friends set out to rescue the victims of the brick kiln, they went up against people plotting the continued success of their criminal enterprise. The owners of the brick kiln who trafficked the workers did not want their business model to be disrupted, because maintaining a coerced labor force was essential to their scheme.

After several meetings with the police and local government authorities, Indian officials conducted an enquiry to determine if the workers were free to leave. I accompanied them to the brick kiln with over a dozen members of our team who had been diligently working on the case. It was a typical hot day in southern India and this was similar to many other cases we had worked on with the police.

The government officials began to interview workers, and they concluded that the traffickers were illegally holding them as slaves. Once the enquiry was underway, I went with a small group of officials to a location outside the kiln where the slaves who had escaped to seek help were waiting while they gave evidence to the enquiry.

Back inside the brick kiln, the traffickers became agitated as the government deemed more and more workers victims. From the traffickers' perspective, like that of plantation owners in the American south in the 1800s, the government was taking their property and the human engine that generated their income. Our attempts at justice were seen as an attack on their prosperity.

These agitated traffickers sent for their friends, associates, other brick kiln owners, and people sympathetic to their interests. Before long, a large mob formed at the kiln's entrance. The enquiry was almost over, and many of the slaves had courageously told their stories to the authorities. The government officials decided that because of the growing crowd, remaining at the kiln was unsafe, and everyone needed to leave immediately. The buses to remove the freed slaves had not yet arrived, and there were not enough seats in the cars to get everyone out of the kiln in a hurry.

Some victims got into the police cars and our team's vehicles, but the mob pressed in and began dragging them out. Over the course of the day, the traffickers had assured everyone that the workers wanted to work there and were free to leave the kiln. Their actions now belied this, as physical force was used to pull the slaves back into the clutches of the traffickers.

The victims began to flee from their traffickers by running in all directions. Many scrambled over the back wall of the facility and ran into the harsh, rural surroundings. Having lost control of the situation, the police started driving toward the exit. As the mob pressed against the cars, our team jumped into the vehicles and tried to flee for safety.

I received a call saying, 'We are under attack!' We raced back to the kiln entrance and found the mob, now numbering several hundred, bashing in the windshields of the cars with bricks. They had pulled the hired drivers from the cars and taken their car keys.

The hostile crowd was yelling and screaming as I got out of my car and moved toward the mob's leaders. I tried to bargain for my team's safe passage, but was unsuccessful. The traffickers knew that if they let us leave, we would just return later for the same purpose.

The police pulled me into one of their cars for safety as the crowd grew more violent. The intensity of the riot grew when the mob sent for kerosene to set the cars alight with us inside. The slaves scattered and we were trapped. The people who came to rescue others now needed to be rescued themselves.

I prayed to the God of justice for help, feeling responsible for each one of my friends as the team leader. The police who were trapped with us were as afraid as we were. Using my mobile phone, I called everyone I could and activated our office's emergency protocol, wondering which would arrive first – the kerosene, or people to help us? The work of justice had just become more difficult as our human adversaries worked actively against us.

Straight-line life

As I sat in that hot car with the angry crowd pressed against it, I reviewed the entire operation. Had we made a mistake? Often, when things do not progress smoothly, many of us think that we are on the wrong track. We assume that if the goal is noble and worthwhile, the path to it should be straight and smooth. Such thinking is flawed.

Living out our calling and purpose is rarely an easy, direct route. Some followers of Jesus in the affluent West think they are entitled to a 'straight-line life' – a safe, smooth path from A to B. The truth is, we are not entitled to anything. Just because things are not working out does not necessarily mean we have gone wrong. Our culture often confuses easy paths with correct paths, and difficult paths with wrong paths.

This journey of justice looks like more of a mountain road than an easy stroll. There are unexpected sharp turns, delays, and even dead ends. Victims die before trial, evidence seems to disappear, and power is sometimes on the side of the perpetrators. One can easily doubt the route because the path makes little sense.

Tianmen Mountain in China's Hunan Province boasts one of the most dangerous roads in the world, with breath-taking hairpin turns. Seen in two dimensions, the track from the bottom of the mountain to the summit looks more like a child's scribble than a well-planned way to make progress to the destination.

Our perspective suddenly changes, however, when we see things in three dimensions. When we understand the topography, the road makes much more sense – a road straight up to the top would never work. The grade would be too steep; the switchbacks are the only way to get to the summit.

History shows that obstacles have confronted the leaders of most great movements. Failure was always a real possibility for William Wilberforce, Mahatma Gandhi, and Martin Luther King. They did not know how things would turn out before they started, but displayed remarkable perseverance through adversity, setbacks, and even death threats. They considered their sacrifices worthwhile to pursue the noble goals of restraining evil and bringing justice. Our team had been inspired by such great leaders.

Conflict clarity

One thing became clear to me as I sat wondering if help would arrive before kerosene. The violence we faced meant that we were on the right track. The traffickers' reactions were proportionate to their commitment to keep their slaves trapped. If our work was not making a difference in the fight against slavery, they would not react with such intensity to their laborers' decisions to work elsewhere.

There have been several tense moments during my career fighting human trafficking, and the siege that day in India was certainly one of them. If I burned to death inside that car, what would my wife and young children do? I was also concerned about our team members and their families who depended upon them. Would people blame me for taking risks? We all struggled with these worries, but encouraged each other during those uncertain moments.

To persevere in this work over the long term, we need to be wise and avoid unnecessary risks. The hard work of justice, however, is punctuated by unavoidable risks. We must engage with the traffickers to restrain them, and those invested in criminal schemes rarely relinquish power voluntarily. Their power to exploit others must be taken from them by the rule of law, and that creates unavoidable conflict.

When it comes to combating human trafficking, there are no neat, tidy, risk-free choices. The one who seeks justice may possibly be harmed, but not working to free victims means certain continued harm. We must accept the risks inherent in the work and take reasonable steps to manage them.

Many of us are taught that confrontation is a negative thing and we avoid conflict because it is uncomfortable, difficult, and has an uncertain outcome. Although conflict can too often result from bad behavior or an unwillingness to get along, at other times confrontation is necessary and even good. To leave evil unchallenged is itself a harm. Not all conflict should be avoided.

Dr. Martin Luther King, Jr., said about the 1955-1956 Montgomery Bus Boycott during the Civil Rights Movement in the United States,

'True peace is not merely the absence of tension; it is the presence of justice.'

When injustice is confronted there will be tension and conflict. But a passive co-existence with injustice allows traffickers to operate with impunity. The unavoidable conflict with our human adversary reminded me that we were on the right track to the noble goal of freedom.

Trapped rescuers

While our caravan was stuck, the mob continued to grow. The sea of people blocked my ability to see the other cars or even the horizon. Off in the distance, however, where the road curved around a hill, I spotted several large trucks coming our way. When I pointed this out to the lead police official in my car, he smiled for the first time all afternoon. The trucks were filled with troops from the reserve police force that had been dispatched to save us from the mob.

The reserve police officers lined both sides of the road and recovered the car keys from the mob. Our cars inched forward as the crowd reached past the police guard and struck our badly damaged vehicles. With the police escort, we drove in line to a police station and the drama was over.

Taking stock, we determined that the injuries to our team were all minor, though everyone was shaken up from the ordeal. Our team was safe, but our mission seemed a failure.

I have never seen such courage and dedication as from my colleagues then. Instead of licking their wounds and getting a good night's sleep, they wanted to go out immediately to seek the scattered slaves. They knew that the traffickers would be looking for them and it was a race to see who would find them first. The slaves had nowhere to go, no supplies, and no provisions. Time was on the side of the well-resourced traffickers.

That was the moment that changed everything. No one would have criticized the men and women on our team if they had gone home after a bad day at work. Their adversary had restricted their movement and threatened their lives.

I wondered if some might resign their positions and look for less risky ways to make a difference. But instead they redoubled their efforts for their neighbors. Our team's passion for justice was accompanied by extraordinary perseverance as they mustered the endurance to finish the job.

The decision to search for the victims after a painful and seemingly decisive setback determined the outcome of that case. Such perseverance will also decide if the system of slavery will be defeated around the globe. The question we must ask ourselves is, 'Do we care more about people we do not even know than the traffickers care about their power? Do we want justice more than traffickers want their illicit profits?'

The dust of the day was caked on our faces with dried sweat. We were hungry, thirsty, and tired. One colleague told me, 'Today we just got a taste of what the victims live with every day.' Seeking justice can mean danger, discomfort, and sacrifice.

My friends were authentic Christians. They walked humbly with their God. Now they were running humbly with their God in an overwhelming demonstration of love in action. Instead of retreating from the hard work of justice and avoiding conflict, my friends faced the problem with an abiding confidence that their cause was just.

I have met many intelligent people around the globe working to fight the crime of human trafficking, some from the most prestigious academic institutions. I have met many people who care deeply about the plight of the oppressed. Their hearts are broken for the people harmed by violence and injustice. I have met people with impressive experience in dealing with public justice systems and victim care. They have spent years working in organizations that deal directly with the problem of human trafficking.

Intelligence, passion, and experience are admirable and necessary traits, but alone they do not sustain the work of justice around the world. The challenge of seeking justice requires an inner resolve that generates perseverance and endurance. Thoughtful, intense effort over time allows justice seekers to outwit and outlast traffickers.

Freedom found

As our team searched for the scattered slaves, the reports from the field began to trickle in to the office. Our team found a few slaves huddled together in a nearby village. Then they found a few more. Within days, all the victims who fled that day were safe and reunited with their families.

After our failed enquiry and the siege of our caravan, the victims had even less reason to believe that the authorities could help them. Their faint hopes for freedom had now been battered by more traumatic experiences. I wondered if they would trust us again after our failed attempt to free them, but my friends convinced them to believe that the law would prevail.

I set a date with the government officials to bring all the victims back so that they could complete the enquiry, but this time at the local courthouse instead of the brick kiln. When we arrived, the government compound was packed with people. The traffickers, and many familiar faces from the mob, were present.

As the enquiry resumed, the cacophony of the traffickers' objections and complaints clanged like cymbals. In stark contrast, the advocates on our team pled the case for justice like the persistent widow, and they prevailed. The judge declared each of the victims 'free people.' Every man, woman, and child working in the brick kiln received a document from the court declaring them free.

The victims' improbable hope for freedom had become a practical reality. Moving from the point A of injustice to the point B of freedom had not been a straight, easy path, as obstacles and difficulties plagued the case. Yet noble men and women persevered to see justice done.

Since then the survivors have been rebuilding their lives with the help of various non-profit groups, while the prosecution of the traffickers is on going. In the months and years following that raid, our team continued to investigate cases and serve victims. We developed better plans to reduce risks and mitigate the chances of riots during enquiries, but the unavoidable risks remain. There is work left to do.

The scourge of modern slavery should motivate us to passionate, thoughtful action. Yet our passion must be paired with perseverance if we are to succeed. Human adversaries make the work of making wrong things right exceptionally hard.

There will be painful setbacks and hardships, but seeking justice for victims remains a worthy battle we must fight to the end. As Dr Martin Luther King, Jr, said at the crescendo of his historic 'I have a dream' speech in Washington, DC, 'The arc of the moral universe is long, but it bends towards justice.'

John Cotton Richmond has worked on the front lines of the global fight against human trafficking for over a dozen years. He pioneered International Justice Mission's human trafficking casework model in India and has prosecuted numerous victim-centered sex trafficking and forced labor cases as a federal prosecutor with the US Department of Justice's Human Trafficking Prosecution Unit. He is a graduate of Wake Forest University School of law and has served as an international expert on human trafficking for the United Nations. He is also a writer and frequent speaker on topics of faith, social justice, vocation, parenting, and human trafficking. You can learn more about John's work at www.johncottonrichmond.com and follow him @JohnRichmond1. The views expressed in this chapter are his own and do not purport to be those of the US Department of Justice or the International Justice Mission.

Chapter 3
iCampaign
Danny Smith

I became aware of modern slavery in the 1980s after reading an article by John Pilger in the *Daily Mirror*, and talking to him about his work as an investigative journalist. Some years later, while attending a mission conference in the Philippines, I decided to probe the sensational stories about slavery that I had heard.

I learned that young girls – many extremely young – were easy to find in the bars around the capital city of Manila. Some were trafficked to Japan by criminal gangs linked to the Yakuza, the Japanese mafia. The gangs used women as recruiters who lured girls to foreign shores with false promises of employment and an enticement to earn money for their families.

Law enforcement and politicians seemed powerless or willfully negligent. It was evident that young girls were enslaved in the sex business, an illegal activity covered by corrupt officials who looked the other way. It was astonishing to learn that foreigners, including UK nationals, were active in the trade, and in the abuse.

The discoveries were disturbing, almost hard to comprehend, but the issue seemed too large, too complex. I didn't want merely to raise awareness about such issues without bringing change, so assumed that our organization (Jubilee Campaign) was too small to make any difference.

Father Shay

In 1992, I met Father Shay Cullen and this was to be a transformative experience. He was challenging the principalities and power-systems in place in the Philippines, and was the first person I'd met who had a convincing overview of what action to take. Significantly, he believed that we as individuals had a part to play. It was a revelation.

Father Shay's parish was Olongapo City, once called the biggest brothel in the world because it had been turned into an adult playground used as 'R&R' by the American military engaged in the Vietnam War. He defended exploited and enslaved women and children, and pursued the offenders with the dogged passion of an Old Testament prophet and a modern-day detective. It was faith in action that I had not experienced before and helped me understand how we find our place in a world aflame with injustice, corruption and turmoil.

With Father Shay, we designed a campaign to target UK nationals who abuse children overseas and get away with it. At the time, men could violate children abroad and video tape the abuse. If, on their return, customs stumbled on them at Heathrow Airport, they would be prosecuted for obscene materials, the videos. The abuse of the child itself was not punishable by British law – madness!

Our campaign strategy was to use the media and Parliament to tackle the issue. Working with David Alton, the Liberal MP for Liverpool, we set up the All-Party Parliamentary Group for Street Children in 1992.

The group's first official meeting in the House of Commons launched our campaign calling on the government to change the law so that British sex tourists who abused enslaved children overseas could be prosecuted in the UK. It was not enough to express pity for the children held as sex slaves for foreigners to jet in and abuse; we had to stop the offenders getting away with it.

Glenda Jackson MP took our 20,000-strong petition to Downing Street, and our parliamentary officer, barrister Wilfred Wong, drafted a bill that went through several twists in the Parliamentary process. The government insisted that our objectives were naïve, impractical and impossible to implement. We were confidently informed that this legislation would never happen, and that our campaign's time and resources would be better utilized elsewhere.

To keep up the pressure we worked on several investigations and one of our operations landed on the front page of the now defunct *News of the World*, the UK's biggest selling newspaper. The exposé identified UK nationals who were active in the sex trade overseas, but were 'untouchable' by British law, and could therefore act with impunity.

Father Shay sent me video footage that showed a foreigner with children as young as six or seven years old on his yacht. The television companies agreed that it would make shocking viewing, but when they learned that the suspect was Australian, their interest plummeted. I was told that only British nationals would make it onto television. This set us on a mission to infiltrate underground groups and 'sex tour' organizers in the UK.

A producer at Independent Television News wrote to me in November 1994 and asked if they could join us on an undercover operation. With ITN involved, the hunt was on to film one of these groups, and expose their activity. I was convinced that if the public could only listen to what we had to say, they would get behind our campaign and insist that the government take a stand.

Undercover

Over several months, I went undercover and secretly recorded conversations with travel agents who offered me sex tours with children available for me to exploit.

One evening, in a Surrey car park, ITN's cameraman disguised a secret camera and recording equipment behind my shirt and loose-fitting jacket. The lens of the secret camera was the size of a button that blended into the complex pattern on a tie that hung around my neck, with the wires carefully hidden from view, but plugged into the electronic devices taped to my body.

The target of this investigation was a travel agent near Chessington's World of Adventures. I had tape recordings of incriminating conversations, but we needed him to confirm this on video without any entrapment or coercion from me. I had convinced him that a face-to-face meeting was essential before I handed over cash for my ticket. He agreed.

I didn't know what would happen after I shut the door and walked in, or how he would react if he discovered the secret camera under my shirt. Perhaps I would be overcome by the intensity of the meeting. But it wasn't difficult to get the sleazebag talking.

'What if I can't find the girls or they're not that young?' I enquired, all recorded on the secret camera. His reply was ominous, but explicit. 'That's not a problem. Just tell me how young you want the girls. Just give me an age. Give me a number.'

Our investigations were featured in reports by ITV News at Ten, *News of the World*, and the *Sunday Mirror*, and confirmed that UK nationals across the country were involved in the sexual exploitation of children overseas.

We also uncovered a college lecturer in London and again, ITN taped me up with a hidden camera and microphone. This time the encounter was in a South London pub. Still, the British government resisted backing such a cause as this. It was perplexing, troubling.

It was different in Ireland, where Father Shay and I raised the need for extra-territorial legislation for sex offences against children. Amidst strategic media coverage and effective lobbying, new legislation went through in November 1995 without much party political maneuvering.

A TV journalist from RTE, Ireland's main television channel, told me that the extraordinary factor was that the government had accepted a private member's bill from the party in opposition – only the fourth in the history of the state. Political opponents put aside disputes and united their forces in the battle against sex tourism and modern slavery. It was a triumph for the campaign.

In the UK, the wall of resistance against introducing this legislation was crumbling. Our political lobbying had intensified, and the media coverage increased. I was sure that change would come; I just didn't know when. Sadly, it would take a tragedy to reach the tipping point.

The killing of Daniel Handley

The disappearance of blond 9-year-old Daniel Handley from the streets of East London in October 1994 created a sensation and his abduction was front page news as the search turned nationwide. When the child's body was found in a shallow grave in Bristol in March 1995, the manhunt intensified. His killers were traced to the Philippines; they had chosen Olongapo City as a hideout.

I was visiting Father Shay when the telephone call came in. The Australian Embassy had responded to a request from Scotland Yard about the fugitives. There was only one man who the Australians could recommend to track down the suspects and it was the Irish priest.

Father Shay's investigators tracked down the suspected killers and Scotland Yard detectives flew out within days to follow up on the evidence he had uncovered. One of the killers had already fled back to the UK and was arrested. But the second man in Olongapo City was caught as a result of the information provided by Father Shay. The suspect was arrested and returned to the UK for a highly publicized trial in May 1996, which eventually saw convictions for both men.

The arrests held particular significance for us. When Scotland Yard caught the killer in the Philippines, he was arrested for immigration violations and for overstaying his visa. More importantly, although he had abused children both in the UK and the Philippines, he was hunted for the crime he had committed in London. His offences against children in the Philippines went unpunished.

The killers of Daniel Handley were both given life sentences as his tragic story carried the most dramatic evidence of how foreigners abused sex slaves overseas. Incredibly, the message was clear: you can abuse children overseas and get away with it.

The increasing media coverage and lobbying, followed by the Irish bill, and finally the Daniel Handley case had created the perfect storm. The government did a sudden U-turn. A low-key dispatch in 1996 announced that extra-territorial legislation for sex offences against children would be incorporated into the 1997 Sex Offenders Act. Much of the legislation was based on the bill that our Parliamentary Officer had drafted two years earlier, and that Lord Hylton had raised in the House of Lords.

The Home Office introduced a sex register for offenders with a proposed three-month penalty and a token fine. It seemed like a slap on the wrist. We worked closely with ECPAT (End Child Prostitution and Asian Tourism) on this campaign and together we lobbied for a stiffer fine, and an increase of six months' imprisonment for failing to register; both measures were successful. Over time, there was further legislation, and pressure on parliament increased.

In 2002, we challenged the UK government to take action on trafficking and called for new laws, since there was no comprehensive legislation to deal with people who were trafficked into the UK, where they were held captive and their abductors controlled all their funds. We asked our supporters to petition the government, and the campaign had an impact.

The Home Office Minister Beverley Hughes MP formally responded to us and said that the government would create a new offence for trafficking (for prostitution) within the Nationality, Immigration and Asylum Bill, and further legislation (in line with the European Union) would be introduced to curb labor and sexual exploitation. We didn't get everything we wanted but it was a start, and demonstrable evidence that campaigning can make a difference.

David Alton, now Lord Alton of Liverpool, initiated one of the first full debates on trafficking, calling for new laws to prevent trafficking. He wrote to encourage our supporters, 'It is always a positive step to have prompted the Government to respond to specific points of action that we have raised. We are delighted at the number of supporters who have taken action – this is proof that ordinary people can make their voices heard. We welcome the Government's stated intention to introduce new legislation on this issue in the next Queen's Speech. We will be holding them to account for this pledge.'

Father Shay had taken me on an unforgettable journey, and there was no turning back. He had demonstrated that we could take a part in bringing change for children at risk. In 1996, we became involved with a remarkable rescue mission in India with Reverend Devaraj of Bombay Teen Challenge, and over time, several hundred girls were rescued from the city's red light district. All would have ended up as 21st century sex slaves if they had not been saved.

Over the next decade, a greater awareness of modern-day slavery emerged as Parliamentarians, churches, activists and non-governmental organizations got involved and we welcomed every support given. Before retiring from Parliament, Anthony Steen introduced the Anti-Slavery Day Bill and it became law in 2010. This legislation defined modern-day slavery as child trafficking, forced labor, domestic servitude and trafficking for sexual exploitation and 18 October was declared Anti-Slavery Day.

Anthony made plans to set up the Human Trafficking Foundation (HTF) and Lord Alton asked me to help; in turn, I drew in Bill Hampson from the Epiphany Trust. Bill and I had our first meeting with Anthony in January 2011 in an empty room in the Mermaid Theatre overlooking the Thames where he had temporary use of a rent-free office. We had our notebooks open on a blank page. Anthony outlined his objectives and told us, 'I want the Human Trafficking Foundation to support and add value to the work of organizations that are doing such good work.'

I suggested to Anthony that the HTF should give recognition to people and initiatives that had made an impact on the issue of slavery and that he should institute a series of annual awards. He liked the idea and tasked Bill and me with organizing the first awards events (for the media) in the House of Lords, which Lord Alton hosted in 2011 on Anti-Slavery Day.

The Prime Minister expressed his support for Anti-Slavery Day and hosted a reception at Downing Street that same year. Mr Cameron declared, 'I'm delighted that so many organizations have taken up the fight against modern slavery. This is an important issue and a priority for this government.'

Bill and I left Number Ten early. To promote Anti-Slavery Day we joined with other groups to host 'Dangerous Songs that Changed the World' to show how the music of African slaves in America had influenced modern popular music.

We held the meeting in South London at Holy Trinity Clapham, the church attended by William Wilberforce which became the nerve center for the abolitionist movement. Lord Alton stepped into the pulpit used by John Newton, the slave trader turned preacher, and launched the landmark event.

I always thought of David as the Wilberforce of our age and there was something particularly inspiring about hearing him speak about modern slavery from that historically significant location. It was also stirring to see the photojournalist Hazel Thompson's powerful images from her investigation for the Body Shop's campaign into trafficking in South Africa before the World Cup.

Slavery can be traced throughout human history. In ancient cultures, slaves were drawn from prisoners of war, but the enslaved weren't defined by color or race; many were European. The transatlantic slave trade transformed our concept of slavery. It became the largest international business of the age, and changed the world beyond anything anyone could imagine.

The slaves of Africa played an important part in establishing a new world order as they provided the labor force that powered a new international financial system. The transatlantic slave trade enriched and developed every slave-trading country, and the slave labor force generated the wealth of European and American nations

Today, the name of Wilberforce creates a surge of dynamism and he is upheld as an example of faith in action. This is as it should be. Wilberforce led the Parliamentary campaign for many years, and spurred other politicians to action. Yet, in our enthusiasm to honor this man, perhaps we have obscured others and diminished some factors that played a significant role in the campaign to end the slave trade.

The transatlantic slave trade ended for several reasons. The slave trade was no longer the reliable and lucrative investment it had once been; the revolts and uprisings amongst the slaves themselves increased and spread fear.

Pressure came from the campaign mounted by the abolitionist movement led by Thomas Clarkson, starting with the Quakers and church groups. It was strongly supported and led by Christian women and reinforced by African slaves themselves, men such as Olaudah Equiano, a towering figure.

Today, sex tourists and traffickers have taken over from yesterday's slave traders. The slaving ships and clippers have been replaced by modern technology: mobile phones, the internet and easy international travel. The traffickers target the dispossessed and powerless, the weak and vulnerable, those trapped in poverty and debt. Slavery is illegal in every country on our planet, yet there are more slaves alive today than all the slaves stolen from Africa over four centuries of the slave trade.

Kevin Bales, one of the leading authorities on modern slavery, estimated that there were 27 million slaves worldwide, a statistic frequently quoted. He defined slavery as one person controlling another; violence being used to maintain that control; and that control being used to exploit people economically.

Working with the Walk Free Foundation, he was the lead author of the Global Slavery Index (GSI), and in 2013 produced a revised estimate that 29.8 million people were enslaved globally; their research ranked 162 countries and listed 10 countries (India, China, Pakistan, Nigeria, Ethiopia, Russia, Thailand, Democratic Republic of Congo, Myanmar and Bangladesh) that accounted for 76% of the total global estimate.

Sex trafficking frequently captures the headlines and has become the subject of dramas, documentaries and projects. Operation Pentameter brought together all police forces to get an understanding of sex slavery in Britain. Their investigation uncovered trafficking rings bringing thousands of girls and women into Britain, mostly East European youth desperate for jobs. Newspapers reported of slave auctions held at Stansted Airport with girls taken directly to British brothels.

Yet the numbers involved in sex trafficking (and other forms of slavery) are insignificant when compared to the statistics of slaves trafficked into debt bondage. Bonded labor is the most common form of modern slavery and the UN's Working Group on Slavery reported that about 20 million people worldwide were affected. In *Disposable People*, Kevin Bales observed that India 'may have more slaves than all the other countries of the world put together' with the majority of slaves being Dalits or 'untouchables.' Dalits comprise nearly one quarter of India's society and constitute the largest number of people who have been categorized as modern-day slaves in any nation on earth. The 2013 GSI estimated that India had between 13,300,000 and 14,700,000 people enslaved through debt bondage and bonded labor.

Kevin Bales contributed a chapter to the book I edited in 2007 (*Slavery Now and Then*) and everyone involved in the struggle against modern slavery can take direction from the title of his essay: 'How we will end modern slavery.' It's a task for all of us. However, let's be clear; there is no single action or group that will end slavery. There is no magic bullet.

In the past, the state was an instigator in the exploitation of oppressed people. Now, criminal gangs, sometimes individuals, have taken the lead. Human trafficking is popular because there are low start-up costs, minimal risks, high profits, an increasing demand. Organized crime prefer trafficking people over drugs and arms for one simple reason: they can be sold and re-sold.

It is encouraging to see church networks and Christian leaders strive to revive that passion of the abolitionist movement and to take up the challenge of Jesus of Nazareth and the call of Scripture to take sides with the poor, the exploited, the oppressed, the fallen, the weak, the broken, the vulnerable, the outsider, the stranger . . . It is our humanity that connects us to others, and our faith that gives a context for our expression of compassion, driven by a restlessness of spirit when we encounter injustice.

Slavery affects every continent of the world and the global panorama of the booming slave trade is becoming a defining issue of our times. But our hearts rise with the warriors of justice who take their place with a renewed sense of purpose and are joining the campaign to expose – and end – slavery in the 21st century.

Danny Smith is the Founder and International Director of Jubilee Campaign, which combines effective lobbying and transformational charitable action for Children at Risk. Jubilee Campaign set up the All Party Parliamentary Group for Street Children and has consultative status at the United Nations.

Contact danny@jubileecampaign.co.uk
www.jubileecampaign.co.uk

Chapter 4
The Mission to End Slavery
Shay Cullen

Slavery saturates society. It is present in the clothes and food we buy which are made with slave-like labor. These products are soaked with the sweat and suffering of their victims. They are for sale in the high street shops, on our dining tables, in the food that we eat, worn by children in school and on the sports fields, and present in the mobile gadgets we use daily. The products of modern-day slavery are ever present, but to see them, we need to be freed from blind ignorance.

The sweatshops of Bangladesh are shocking examples of some of the twenty million trafficked humans in slave-like conditions worldwide. Hundreds have died in factory fires and inside five-storey, poorly constructed buildings which collapsed on them as they made the clothes we love to wear. The cocoa fields of Africa and the gold mines of Peru are slave pits where the poor are working in subhuman conditions for less than a survival allowance, and some for none at all.

We might think that slavery ended with the American civil war, or when it was banned by the British parliament through the work of great Christian campaigners against slavery, like William Wilberforce and Thomas Clarkson and their supporters.

For thousands of years, slavery was common practice; it was condoned and a source of revenue for most religions. Churches and the ruling elite of England, Spain, Portugal, Denmark and others, in cahoots with plantation managers and the ruling families of the Americas, all grew rich on the slavery of the captured and enslaved Africans and native peoples.

Humans have a propensity to dominate and exploit their weaker and vulnerable fellow humans. Sadly, history shows that so-called Christians did it with harsh and cruel torture, some while reading the Bible. That Christians could enthusiastically embrace slavery to enrich themselves, was and is a mind-boggling contradiction.

The modern slavery behind much international trade and in our everyday products calls us to question our understanding and practice of our faith. The most vigorous stand against slavery was taken by the Quakers, to their great credit.

In the past, church-going slavers, ship captains, and their financial backers paid lip service to the teachings of Jesus of Nazareth. Shameless hypocrisy was worn with pride. Today, secular society has more openly rejected and ignored Christ's words and example. As a result, thinly disguised modern slavery, as found in brothels, for example, has a sheen of legality. The trafficking of persons that supplies the victims is generally ignored or dealt with lightly in many countries.

There is arguably as little compassion, social and economic justice and equality today as in days when slave ships brought the African captives to the Americas and returned back with the produce of their labor: sugar, cotton, tobacco, gold. There are as many, if not more, exploited and trafficked workers disguised as legitimate employees today, as in the past.

As many as thirteen million Africans were captured, chained, beaten, abused, and enslaved. They were transported like animals and perhaps 1.3 million died on the way in the fetid holds of the slave ships, designed and built to hold as many chained prisoners as space would allow. Their families were torn apart; they were agonizingly separated from wives and children, exiled to the American colonies and their horrific slave plantations to provide products for Western capitalism and commerce for European citizens.

The wealth of much of Europe was founded on the labor of enslaved Africans. Churches built in the 19th century were possible because of slave trade earnings, which is truly a shame and abomination. All prospered at the expense of the enslaved people. They rejoiced in the fruits of slavery and thanked God for their wealth and so-called 'good fortune.' What God did they worship?

Today, as many as 20 million people are trafficked into forced, unpaid labor or on the dollar-a-day survival menu. Slavery has not gone away. The greed for riches produced by enslaving our fellow humans, exploiting them along with the murderous trade in arms and chemical weapons, and life-destroying drugs dominates our global trade. It is clear that governments with a human rights protection agenda are not doing nearly enough, and are having little impact.

True Christians must step into the gap, take a stand and campaign for the gospel values to change society and end slavery. What greater cause than to work for an end to social and racial injustice, bonded labor and slavery and the trade in persons? Putting faith into action is a life worth living; anything else is indifference and apathy in the face of evil.

The peace and compassion, freedom and dignity, championed by Jesus are ideals that give purpose and meaning to human existence. Slavery of any kind by any means is a deprivation of what makes us preciously human: thoughtful free choice. When this unique attribute that sets us apart from all other living creatures is taken from us, our human dignity is diminished, our rights are denied, and we are being treated as less than human.

That's why the captivity that goes with human trafficking is devastating to human beings. Their self-esteem is taken from them and their will to live is weakened. Many turn to suicide. Without the freedom to choose, to exercise free will, to decide for oneself how and where to live without the chains of debt, paralyzing fear and threats, the helpless captive is reduced to the state of the silent caged bird, the chained whimpering puppy.

When Jesus declared in his home town that his mission was to fulfill the promise and prophecy of Isaiah to uplift the poor, open the minds and hearts of those blinded by tradition and ignorance, and declare a Jubilee year where all captive slaves would be freed and debts be cancelled and forgiven, and land would be returned to its rightful owners, there was an angry uproar from the elders, landowners and the wealthy.

His veiled message was clear to the astute teachers of the law and the biblical scholars. To them he was going to turn the power structure of society on its head, deliver it to the poor and the downtrodden and give power to the freed slaves. The rich were outraged, and the poor were delighted.

The mission statement of Isaiah was adopted word for word by Jesus. In the synagogue of Nazareth, he was invited to read the scripture. He opened the scroll, looked for the passage from Isaiah and read:

> The Spirit of the Lord is upon me, because he has chosen me to bring the Good News to the poor. He has sent me to proclaim liberty to the captives, and recovery of sight to the blind: to set free the oppressed and announce that the time has come when the Lord will save his people. (Luke 4:16-19).

No wonder the authorities were outraged. What an audacious, arrogant statement to make! We can imagine their response: 'Who is this son of a carpenter to claim he is equal to the great Isaiah and that he would implement and fulfill the prophet's mission?'

This was pure fantasy if not blasphemy to them. But it was also dangerous and subversive. Talk of freeing captives and slaves was treason to the Romans, and the proxy rulers of Palestine feared losing their religious power and wealth if they lost their positions.

The slave rebellion of Spartacus only a hundred years previously in 73 BC and two previous uprisings of hundreds of thousands of slaves terrified the Romans, as their economy was run on slave labor. It was much like today's world, run on the bonded labor of twenty million people.

To the ruling elite of Palestine, Jesus was an upstart, self-appointed preacher, teaching without any official authority and challenging the traditional teaching of Judaism.

The poor were taught by the Pharisees and teachers of the law that the power structure and religious elite was God's will. They were told to accept their poverty and slavery as punishment because they were sinners and beyond redemption. Or perhaps they were suffering for their parents' sins. The rich considered that their wealth was God's reward for their virtue and righteousness.

Jewish rabbis spoke of a vengeful and unforgiving God. A sinner or defiled person could make atonement to God if he could afford to make sacrifices in the temple. This required him to buy the animals from the herds of the rich, and give the sacrificed dead carcass to the temple priests who in turn supplied the meat market at great profit. The rich landowners and the priestly caste had a clever, vertically integrated enterprise going on between them.

Besides that they ran a foreign exchange business inside the temple to facilitate the purchase of animals by the Jews returning from foreign lands. They were enraged when Jesus said it was all wrong and he would sweep it all away. They considered him a dangerous heretic, dragged him from the building and tried to kill him by throwing him from a cliff. Somehow he walked away.

But he always made it clear that he was not going to sweep tradition and the law away, he was going to fulfill it, and it would not be instant. Because people had free will to do good or evil, to choose to have their eyes opened to the truth and repent. That would take time. It is still taking time.

Slavery was common in every town and village of Palestine at the time of Jesus as it was in the Roman Empire. No one thought there was anything wrong with it. But Jesus did. He would probably be killed on the spot by the Romans for openly opposing it. After quoting the words of Isaiah, he was a marked man.

Advocating openly for equality and freedom for the captives and the poor was a dangerous mission. Jesus' challenge to the system and denunciation of corrupt hypocrites eventually led to his execution.

While the Sermon on the Mount was a powerful social and spiritual declaration for the rights of the poor, he taught most forcibly by example. He related as a concerned friend to the downtrodden and the rejected. It established before the world their worthiness as God's children and their inalienable rights to be free from all bondage, imprisonment, domination and control by others.

'Whatever you do to the least of my brothers and sisters you do to me,' was another statement identifying with the captives, the slaves. He taught us and gave us the choice to imitate his example. He established their status as God's children with equal rights irrespective of wealth, age, gender, color or creed. All were deserving of freedom, equality, a life of decency based on justice and compassion, love and truth.

He turned upside down the status quo of society of his time and for all time and favored those who had no standing in society. When asked who in his kingdom was the most important of all he choose a child. 'Whoever welcomes this child welcomes me,' he declared to all. This was so shocking in his day that he made enemies.

Even the early Christians struggled with slavery; it was commonly accepted, an unquestioned way of life. They couldn't change the system but now after two thousand years of Christianity, you would think the message of Jesus would have come through to modern society. Yet only a small band of committed anti-slavery advocates champion the rights of the exploited poor who have fallen into the hands of modern-day traffickers and merchants of vulnerable persons.

More of us have to stand up and see our faith in the words and deeds of Jesus of Nazareth in a new light. We have to shake off the old institutional model of religion that passed for Christianity, become true disciples, and join the prophetic voices calling for freedom from slavery for all.

There are strong prophetic voices of people putting faith into action. This book is one of them. As James wrote in the New Testament, 'Faith without action is dead.' We cannot be fully mature Christians if we remain in our church pews without going out to confront the evil of slavery in society. Some are doing it with great effect.

Most uncaring officials would never even consider slavery a political or policy issue. In fact, local governments in the Philippines and elsewhere give business permits to sex bar operators linked to the international sex Mafia. In these slave camps, the chains are invisible debts and threats where women and children are victims of sex slavery of one kind or another.

But that is changing, thanks to the impact of the anti-slavery advocates. The United States government under President Obama has taken on the issue to end the trafficking in persons and modern-day slavery with vigor and commitment.

I never thought this would be so. When I began this work forty years ago, it was because the US Navy made Subic Bay, Olongapo and Angeles City their home port and airfields. Together with the local ruling political family, they developed these villages into huge, exploitative sin cities where sex slavery was and still is as common as selling meat in the market.

An anti-slavery, anti-child abuse campaign by Preda Foundation from 1982 to 1992 succeeded with others to drive the US military bases from the Philippines – with some help from the eruption of Mount Pinatubo. Although the slavery business shut down for a few years, it has since been restarted by returning US retired marines and an international sex Mafia. Now sex tourists fill the brothels and bars. With the help of the Almighty we were able to get rid of the huge US military bases, so there is great hope that we can get rid of sex tourism in the Philippines and save thousands of enslaved young girls, women and children.

The battle is spiritual. We need the influence of Eternal Goodness to conquer the hearts and minds of enough politicians, to legislate for clean tourism that is safe for women and children, and against modern forms of slavery. We need an international campaign where Christians of courage and commitment take an active stand for what they believe. Prayer is great, but action for justice is greater still.

Until very recently, no one thought that in our time, still soaked in racism and prejudice, we would see a black president in the White House, a seat of awesome power, built with slave labor. He and his wife Michelle, herself a descendant of slaves, have been advocating an end to slavery as a matter of state policy and priority. Transformational social and moral change is possible with great spiritual commitment to human rights and dignity.

The latest Trafficking in Person (TIP) report, released and publicized on 20 June 2014 by the US Secretary of State John Kerry, stated that trafficking of persons is modern slavery and its eradication is a top-priority policy for all US government departments.

Who would have foretold that the US government would do this? The former administration was advocating policies to invade, fight and kill, conquer and occupy. So we welcome this amazing change of policy.

There has been nothing much like it in government since William Wilberforce and Thomas Clarkson, where former slaves Ottobah

Cugoano and Olaudah Equiano and their supporters campaigned for many years to abolish slavery and challenged the British Parliament to do so. Eventually the campaigners persuaded MPs to ban the slave trade. The Slave Trade Act received Royal Assent on 25 March 1807 and many years later slavery itself was outlawed, just three days before William Wilberforce died.

There are many forms of slavery. It is the physical control of another human being, making him or her work for little or no pay and controlling their behavior from dawn to dusk.

There are also addictions where the human will is dominated by chemical substances or other compulsive behaviors. The drug traffickers and pushers trap, enslave and destroy young lives. There is intellectual slavery where people's minds, feelings and spirits are captured and controlled by an ideology and their will is no longer free. Some can become fanatics, even suicide bombers.

The fight against human trafficking is one of the greatest challenges we have to face this century. Yes, we have wars, famine, typhoons, massacres and climate change. But I believe that Christians must face the problem of evil epitomized in the slavery of the poor and vulnerable people who are left unprotected by family and community.

The inevitable question for people of faith is, 'If there is a loving, all-powerful God who cares for us, why does evil thrive to enslave the innocent, especially women and children and cause them to suffer?'

There is no easy answer to this but I have grappled with it and sought answers all my life. I found that action for justice against evil and slavery helped me live with the many challenges to my faith. Reggie and Angelica are just two of many.

A few months ago, after the devastating typhoon Haiyan that hit the Philippines, hunger was rampant. People would do anything for food. The youth were easily exploited by human traffickers.

Preda Foundation social workers rescued Reggie, a teenager who was lured with his six friends on board a fishing boat and were exploited as slave labor. They worked for weeks without end for sixteen hours a day and were then cast ashore without pay or compensation.

Sixteen-year-old Reggie, as if he had not suffered enough, was then arrested for 'vagrancy,' for being homeless. The police didn't believe him or were in cahoots with the slavers and exploiters, the traffickers of Reggie and his friends who went off to exploit more minors on their fishing boat, a slave ship of sorts. He told us later he felt that God had abandoned him.

There are about ten million homeless people in despicable slums, living in pushcarts on the streets all over the Philippines; they are prisoners of poverty, another kind of slavery. Preda human rights workers demanded the release of Reggie from illegal detention and succeeded in getting him out. There were dozens of other small boys in the same cells arrested and accused of theft for stealing a banana, a T-shirt, or some petty offences, some as young as ten years old. We could not rescue all of them.

In the jail house they endure hardship and are forced into another form of slavery. Like other boys, Reggie was bossed by the bigger inmates and had to be their unpaid servant. Some are turned into girly-boys, forced to give sexual favors to the guards or adult prisoners in adjoining cells. Young girls are also sold as sex slaves to the older adult prisoners to appease their cravings and prevent riots.

These victims of abuse work without pay. Boys and girls wash the guards' clothes, clean the filthy toilets, cook and serve food, and do whatever they are ordered just to eat and avoid being beaten up. They are totally impoverished so no one cares about them.

Reggie was released into the custody of the Preda human rights workers and had his first meal in a restaurant. He was then brought to the Preda home in the countryside to rest and recover his broken health.

During the sharing of testimony, he told his story of exploitation and suffering and what he witnessed in the jail. He also described his journey in Christian faith and hope: 'I only had God to trust and prayed to God to save me. I hoped every day would be the day when I would be saved, but my prayers were unanswered.'

The worst of all human traffickers and slavers are those who recruit children and young women and sell them into sex slavery. These are the government-approved, licensed brothels and sex bars operated by the international sex Mafia which bring in sex tourists from all over the world. Fourteen-year-old Angelica was sold to a trafficker by her relatives and ended up a sex slave in the 'Sweet Sixteen Bar' that specialized in minors. When we rescued her from that sex bar where she endured a year of suffering, she told us she was forced to take customers six times a night and she begged God for deliverance.

'I prayed and begged for God to save me, to take me out of that place, to bring me safely home.' That child was deeply traumatized by sex slavery. She hated adults, trusted no one and it took almost a year of counseling and emotional expression therapy before she could heal and trust again.

Many survivors of sexual exploitation and abuse live with that deep distrust of other humans. It's a lonely life not being able to have close friends and happy relationships.

It is not God who is ignoring the horrific suffering of these enslaved people. It is those who claim to be Christians but are not, who abandon them to the abusers and slavers. All of us are challenged and called to be Good Samaritans but most walk on by, so the bandits win and the innocent suffer.

Eternal Goodness does not allow or ignore human suffering; people do. Eternal Goodness is present when there are good people acting for justice and love and personifying it. True Christians are those who act on their faith, extending the mission of Jesus of

Nazareth in the world. Together in his spirit, and that of Isaiah, people of faith combat evil.

We wouldn't be truly human without the freedom to exercise free will, nor could we choose to help, love and save others. So evil is not allowed by God, but for humans to be fully human, they must have the freedom to choose to do good or evil. It is for Christians to present eternal goodness and eliminate evil.

More people in the world seem to choose wrongdoing than doing good, which is why bad things happen to innocent people. Slavery is the result of the evil choice of traffickers and abusers.

I believe that 'Eternal Goodness' did come through the Preda human rights workers in saving Reggie and Angelica and many more children with the help of our supporters. Their prayers were answered at last.

All of us are called to act as did the Good Samaritan, to help the victims of slavery and bind up their wounds and care for them. As disciples of Christ, our calling is to implement and live out in action that mission statement of Isaiah as Jesus did. We can eventually end slavery by working together with caring people who believe in him and his mission.

Father Shay Cullen is a Missionary priest from Ireland and a member of the Missionary Society of St Columban and Founder and President of Preda Foundation, Philippines. He has worked protecting women and children from sex slavery and promoting human rights, peace and non-violence in the Philippines since 1969. Father Shay is an international speaker, human rights campaigner and the author of Passion and Power, an autobiography. He has been nominated three times for the Nobel Peace Prize and received other human rights awards. He resides at the Preda Foundation, Upper Kalaklan, Olongapo City, Philippines and reached at shaycullen@preda.org.

Chapter 5
Hiding in Plain Sight:
Pattaya, Thailand 2001
Rebecca and Clint Dunning

We'd never even heard the term human trafficking. Few talked about modern-day slavery and certainly not in ways that displayed the underbelly of such a practice. We had no idea that it involves more than 27 million souls world-wide, more than the entire 400 years of the transatlantic slave trade combined, if you can believe it.

It was July 2001 and we were invited to be part of a team to serve the missionaries our church had sent out to various places in the world. Scores of us descended on Pattaya, Thailand, which is an hour's bus ride north of Bangkok, to stay at a 4-star resort on the Gulf of Thailand. We were there to love on friends serving in hard places and debrief from our ten-day trip to Delhi, India. After enjoying the luxuries offered at the buffets, beach and swimming pools we decided to catch a taxi and do some shopping in the markets downtown.

While walking around haggling for knock-off products and other touristy items, we grew tired of being assaulted on all sides by young women urging us to come in for massages. We commented in passing to each other that perhaps the women were really selling sexual favors, but had no idea that we were in a red light district famous for offering young women for sexual exploitation.

Yet we began to clue in when we saw American and European men, twice or three times the age of these young beautiful women, out and about shopping as if they were on a date. After asking a few missionaries about it, we were filled in on the horrendous activity going on. Both of us were appalled that once again America in all of its wealth was heaping depravity on the shores of a nation with so much poverty. And little did we know that it was happening in our very own city back home, every single day.

That day, the image that has been forever frozen in our minds emerged. We took our two young children to McDonalds for lunch to check out how the Thai would serve up a Big Mac and some fries. Across the restaurant we saw a young girl receiving her lunch in the form of a Happy Meal from her 'date.' This young girl was so excited about the toy prize inside that she was jumping up and down in her provocative woman's dress, giggling with delight.

Rebecca's story: Restoring the heart

It took all I had to restrain myself from physically attacking the man who had purchased that precious girl and her meal for the day.

I'm ashamed to admit I knew so little of the reality of what was going on when it had been hiding in plain sight for my entire life. I basically knew stereotypes and what media had taught me, even though I'd been raised among women and a couple of men who'd been 'living the life,' some of them close friends. At that time, I thought that people chose prostitution through a series of unfortunate events, bad choices and horrible taste in men. Sure, I thought that poverty and bad childhoods had something to do with it for many.

However, all the women I'd known in the United States in the sex industry growing up (ex-porn stars and women who had been prostituted via escort services and working the street) seemed to be independent, willing, seemingly enjoying it or at least doing it to feed their drug habit. I didn't realize that almost every single person being prostituted had been abused at young ages; many then being in the foster care system and lured by 'Daddy-Boyfriends' into a world that devoured them the second they slipped a toe into its murky waters.

I didn't see the false bravado that was necessary just to get through another day or that the boyfriend that was acting as both abusive and 'loving' pimp. The fact is that as many as 2.8 million children run away each year in the US. Within forty-eight hours of hitting the streets one-third are lured or recruited into the underground world of prostitution and pornography, with the average age being twelve to fourteen for girls and eleven to thirteen for boys.

Breaking through my stereotypes

Despite my naivety in 2001, that McDonalds experience was a moment of awakening where I was forever changed. By 2004 terms like 'social justice' and human trafficking' began to swirl in the conversations of all of us 20-somethings in the church. Statistics rolled off people's tongues in almost any conversation as awareness campaigns began.

Various organizations like Love146 and Stop the Traffik were beginning to bring awareness and Clint and I began to devour the materials, watch the documentaries and read books. Bono became our hero, and we began to pray.

I had always prayed about injustice from my youngest memories. Before I even followed Jesus, I would weep and cry out for God to help people that I saw on television or read about. I'd always felt I'd been born in the wrong time period, fantasizing about being involved in women's suffrage, marching peacefully with Martin Luther King Jr. in the civil rights movement or acting as a conductor in the Underground Railroad in the original abolitionist movement.

I was unaware that I would be presented with my own opportunity to, according to Proverbs 31:8, 'be the voice of those who cannot speak for themselves,' right now in modern history.

Small beginnings

Clint and I were working in clothing design and distribution with a business called Ephod Clothing. We began our own small campaign, 'Clothing with a Cause' that raised awareness and funds for organizations working in intervention and restoration. We still didn't know what we were supposed to do, where to begin, or how to get involved. It seemed so big and overwhelming and we seemed so, well, small and normal.

My big 'aha' moment was when we watched a documentary called *Call and Response*, with musicians and actors creating a soundtrack to get the word out about modern-day slavery. Justin Dillan who spearheaded the project said something along the lines of, 'I knew I had to do something. I couldn't do everything, but had some role to play. I figured I do music, so somehow I can use my talent to touch this issue.'

That was it for me, my takeaway from the movie. I knew I had some small talent that I could use to do a little something. I made a list of what I enjoy doing. I love to gather people, to climb mountains and to write. I figured maybe something could come of it.

In 2009 and 2010, as I published two different children's books, instead of having book launch parties only for me, we started *Justice Speaks: Artists Collaborating to End Modern Day Slavery*. We held them in public forums and had a mishmash of fine art, music, spoken word and other entertainment with a sprinkling of awareness about the atrocities of slavery.

Thank God, we know a lot of talented musicians who were willing to donate their time and talents because we didn't have two nickels to rub together to finance it. We also brought in vendors selling international goods who donated a portion of their proceeds to anti-trafficking causes, and art made by people who'd formally been exploited.

A talented young man shot a video that we then used to get the word out even more. These events have been taken over by a friend, here in Kansas City, Missouri and while it is still organic, she has grown them beyond what we had imagined.

In 2012, we asked each of our three children to choose a child to sponsor through Compassion International. After hearing the statistics about how empowering children and providing love, prayer, nourishment and education greatly reduces their chances of being lured into this form of profiteering, we felt it was a no-brainer. It was a way to join with our kids in this fight without bringing them into the raunchy details of its practices. Even if we never meet our sponsored children personally, our children write to them and we're hoping it makes all the difference in their lives.

Not knowing what else to do, we continued to pray and see where God would lead. It has felt long, as if we were sitting around waiting while women and children were living and dying in hell on earth. I felt like a sell-out just giving small amounts of money to organizations that were 'doing the stuff.'

Getting trained up

In the meantime, I trained in a few healing modalities, received certification and entered into an internship with a woman with ten-plus years of experience, to learn about ministering to survivors of complex trauma.

At first, when I began to meet with women, both to facilitate healing and learn from my mentor, I held back sobs as I heard their stories. Now I sit with them and cry at times, because I'm only human, but am better able to be a safe place for them to share sometimes for the first time the details of their captivity and enslavement.

I've been on my own journey the last couple of years alongside them. Sometimes their pain triggers my pain and causes me to look at the lingering effects of the years of abuse I received in my childhood. I've also realized that it's easy to receive 'vicarious trauma', to be violated in your soul through hearing details of their abuse.

Due to confidentiality, I've had to learn the fine line of how and what to share about what I hear, but in the end have found Jesus to be the greatest Listener, Counselor and the one who carries my burdens and theirs. One thing I know, my heart is as important as the work I do and that it is worth both my and his attention.

What I've learned

What I realize now after a nine-year journey into this work, is that Jesus *was and still is* establishing in us several key things to protect us in the work. First and foremost, our identity comes from being his beloved son and daughter, not from the work or cause we are a part of. When activism becomes our identity, we are in enormous trouble.

Secondly and also essential, is the knowledge that he alone brings justice, not me. Hopelessness, anger and fear will grow like towering weeds in the garden of our lives, if we aren't aware that he is on it, he is able and he is more passionate about it than we are.

The last point has come slower to me, perhaps because of my own story or my tendency towards black-and-white thinking: a heart of mercy for the perpetrator. Here's my conclusion; no six-year-old boy woke up and decided that when he grew up, he wanted to be addicted to porn and buying or selling women and children, just like no little girl dreamed of the cycles of addiction and exploitation. Nevertheless, I am an advocate of incarceration for those who buy men, women and children or sell them.

Boystown, you have my heart

In October of 2012, I received my first invitation to go to Boystown in Reynosa, Mexico. Boystown is a walled area set aside as a zone of tolerance, or sanctioned red light district, by the Mexican government and run by the cartel. Drugs are legal and women can be bought presently for 7.50 US dollars.

My friend, whose name I won't mention for her protection, loves the men, women and children on the border of McAllen, Texas, and had worked there long term until cartel violence led the team to push pause on living in the area. I was invited on a 'scouting' trip to see if Jesus was opening the door to re-establish a full-time presence there again. I went and fell in love with that dark, dank walled city filled with hopeless souls.

On trips, we spend time with Jesus in rhythms of worship and listening prayer each morning. We hear what he wants us to pray and say and then we go and do it.

We often find ourselves praying Isaiah 62 among other verses while we walk the dusty, smelly streets in the Mexican heat, asking him to reveal himself to these lovely ones who are 'called to be a royal diadem with a new name in the hand of our God.' We sing and laugh our way through the poverty-infested areas and pray for the sick and broken as we pass.

We rest and have lunch and then go in small groups into Boystown and meet our friends, who are nothing more than a number on a door to the men purchasing their bodies and using them for fleeting pleasure. Our friends tell us they have no one to laugh and cry with, so we sit in their small rooms and laugh and cry with them as they share their stories.

You would not believe the stories they have to tell, like being transported in a box attached to the bottom of a semi-truck with little to no air, or watching their cartel boyfriend being hauled off to be murdered after being beaten in front of her by his cartel brothers. After listening, we hold them and ask how we can pray, leave them Bibles if they want them, and offer hope for a new life. It doesn't seem like enough.

To meet new girls and begin friendships we bring in 'hope bags,' which are filled with beauty products and toiletries. Sometimes they angrily refuse them, sometimes they grab them and flee and sometimes they cry and open up their stories to us. I consider it a great honor when a girl shares her real name with us instead of the name she uses for anonymity or safety.

Our nights are spent praying and debriefing our day and meeting with women who have come out, sometimes after twenty and thirty years of degradation and crack addiction. One family was living and working in Boystown for three generations and now is living outside the walls. They shine with the love of Jesus and weep over his kindness.

That is when I realize that I am the one who is poor and that Jesus actually brought me to sit at their feet and learn from those who outwardly have little but are much richer than I.

Next January, a full team is moving to Reynosa to establish a work for the women and their children where they will be safe, restored and given skills to begin new lives. Though I won't be moving with the team, I've committed to an advisory role for the work being established and will continue to help gather and train teams heading down for the short-term visits we go on.

Clint's Story: Rescuing the heart

Seeing a man in his fifties buy a young teenage girl a child's meal was offensive in so many ways. A father should take his daughter out for lunch and teach her she's beautiful, not violate her. It wasn't only the age difference or why they were there, but the manipulation of situation.

It was a clear picture of the spirit of this age to destroy the role of a man and a father. If that wasn't the enemy showing his hand, I don't know what was. As I watched him, I saw a smirk on his face that seemed so perverse. In that moment I didn't know what to do.

I realized a basic lunch with my family had turned into something else altogether and it was overwhelming. The world shifted for me as I walked through the district and began to connect all of the dots about what was happening in this area.

My initial feelings for the man, the girl and the district were hopelessness. I didn't know it at the time, but I'd been marked. Hope would come later in my process, but I'd been marked all the same.

The next step

While I was on the trip to India and Thailand, my heart began to be awakened by the Father to my identity as his son and the journey I was called to as a man. I began to see for the first time that all of the adventure I'd longed for was possible. I was coming alive and receiving clarity as I began to see that the rescue of the heart of women and children was something I would do, even if I didn't know what that would look like.

Psalm 18, my favorite scripture, came to mind and connected with this work to fight modern day slavery. It is all about God as a rescuer and how he trains us for this battle as well.

There was so much buzz about social justice and I noticed people couldn't stop talking about it. I decided I didn't just want to add more words to the discussion, but wanted to put action to it. As an artist I thought I could use my skills to at least make a start.

I tend to think very practically and wanted to give it a go with what I had in my possession. I believe that if you take practical action, your daydreams will eventually become your reality. It seems that stewarding the small beginning well is the only way to bring about your dreams; the mundane and monotonous really do matter.

So as a beginning, I created fine art and clothing pieces about justice and apathy. I had always enjoyed writing spoken word, so in addition to art shows, threw down some lines and would grab the mic and pray that hearts were moved when they heard me shout it out. My favorite part was when people who didn't even follow Jesus would be overcome with tears as something they couldn't describe hit them.

Without a heart of mercy for both the perpetrator and the survivors of modern day slavery, you will be left with only anger and defeat. I hate the injustice, but the good news of Jesus is mercy to the most wicked of the wicked, including me.

Team Abolition

In addition to our other ventures, we formed a small group we dubbed 'Team Abolition' and found friends with similar interests to run races, climb mountains and do other crazy adventures, wearing red running jerseys emblazoned with 'Abolitionist' and other information about slavery. We found sponsors. Rebecca began to write articles about our races for the *Gazette* and *Pikes Peak Parent* in Colorado Springs, as well as 24-7prayer.com and The Justice Run.

When we showed up twelve deep, including children, for The Justice Run in Denver, Colorado, which was a fundraiser for a safe home for slavery survivors, other runners would ask about what an abolitionist was. Many had originally just shown up to enjoy another 5 or 10k run but were drawn to the bright red jerseys, signifying our desire to see an end to red light districts world-wide. Several we talked to were inspired for the first time to run the race for a new reason.

Fast forward: 2014

We both have taken on roles in an organization based here in Kansas City, Missouri. The ministry focuses on a number of things, including media, prevention, intervention, restoration and more. Intervention outreach takes place in teams of three: two women and a man meeting with those being sold on our most notorious circuits in the city.

Again the hope bags, with beauty products and toiletries, are handed out along with a hotline number, while trying to establish relational connections. The goal is to create on-going friendship and lifelines for when they find themselves in trouble or are ready to leave the life. Clint's role is to love these beautiful souls, but first and foremost to ensure the safety of the women on his team from pimps and 'customers.'

This ministry also conducts outreach to those being sold on-line. After much patience and assurance that we are not police or another person recruiting them to use them, they agree to meet in a public place. When these women meet up to receive their beauty bag, Clint is the guy reading the newspaper across the restaurant, with a birds-eye view of what is going down. He goes early and leaves after ensuring the team's safety, ready to enter the situation as needed, should a pimp or boyfriend show up or things get out of hand.

Rebecca also works in restoration with women who have chosen to leave the life and follow Jesus. It's hard to describe how much courage it takes to leave what is for many the only thing they've ever known, or the deep-rooted hold of an abusive man.

Restoration is the reknitting and healing of all that has been lost, stolen, given away and decimated. It's not glamorous, but it is really worthwhile. It's also a full-time team effort that includes babysitting, running errands, exercise, nutrition and so on.

These women often need to learn basic life skills such as parenting, getting qualifications, how to dress for an interview and how to clean their living space, not to mention learning to live life without drugs and alcohol. These women meet weekly for scheduled counseling and prayer but run into the realities of their pain on a daily basis. Try to picture living your life as an adult when you are emotionally a pre-teen or young teenager.

Where do we see it going?

We still dream ... We dream of someday personally opening homes for men, women and children coming out of sexual exploitation. These dreams include rescuing hearts and seeing their greatest pain turned into intimacy with the living, loving Father, amidst learning relational skills by being in close proximity to others.

We want them to not just learn life skills like how to create a resume and cook, but to learn how to thrive again and enjoy art and laughter, and to be empowered to give of themselves in healthy ways to their communities.

Mostly, though we both dream of raising our family, loving people well and continuing doing practical things, and having a lot of fun along the way.

Clint and Rebecca Dunning are based in Kansas City, USA and are abolitionists and minister to those working in Boystown (brothel town) Mexico.

Chapter 6
Fighting Slavery
Ben Cooley

When I set up the anti-trafficking charity Hope for Justice, I didn't imagine cycling in my future. It's not the first thing that comes to mind. However, in May 2013 I found myself in Germany gazing up at (what felt like) an enormous mountain, with the prospect of having to cycle up it. I had already cycled through Latvia, Lithuania, Poland and half of Germany in the last ten days, and I was exhausted, in pain and completely certain that I. HATE. CYCLING.

A year before I'd been sitting around a table with our team and my friend Tom Lister, discussing fundraising possibilities. We wanted to do something big that would enable us to expand our operations in the UK, and tackle the horrendous exploitation that is human trafficking. We settled on cycling, but we wanted something special that would be meaningful for us. Therefore I suggested going from Latvia to Southampton, tracing the journey of Zoe, a girl we rescued from sexual exploitation. However, my geography wasn't quite up to scratch, as I thought Latvia was somewhere next to France. FALSE. It's about 40 miles away from Russia.

And so, a year later, I was staring in horror at this mountain, wet, cold and exhausted. You can tell yourself all the way through that you are doing this for those people who are still trapped in horrendous circumstances, enslaved, and that as great as my pain is, it's nothing like theirs. However, when you are actually faced with something that seems insurmountable, and you feel you can't go on, that resolve can leak away.

At this point someone shoved a camera in my face and me asked how I was feeling. I didn't have an answer that didn't involve swearing, so instead I started to sing: 'If faith can move a mountain, let the mountains move.' I looked round in great expectation, but no, it was still there. I sang it again, with my eyes tightly shut and willing that mountain to move with every fibre of my being. It didn't budge.

As hard and painful as it was, I did get up that mountain, and all the way to Southampton. The money we raised from the challenge enabled us to set up Zoe's Hub, our second investigative hub in the UK. Sometimes we sit and wait in faith for circumstances to change, for obstacles to be moved out of our way. But sometimes we need to have faith that we will be able to overcome them. The aim of Hope for Justice is to see the end of slavery. I won't tell you how many people have said to me that this is naïve and ridiculous, and that it will never happen. But it's not just a slogan for us, it's what we are really aiming for, every day. Sometimes it seems too hard, when we've had a difficult case, or we're struggling against a system we can't seem to change; there have been times when I've wanted to give up. But we press on anyway, because every single person who finds freedom from slavery is worth it. We look up at where want to get and start pedaling.

When we got to the end of day eleven of the challenge, I was really ready to give up. There had been steep climbs, bad weather conditions and I'd been sick six times. Tom stopped the whole team because he noticed I was weaving about on the road and shaking. We stopped and had something to eat, then continued a bit slower.

Tom was keeping an eye on me, worried that I might wobble into the path of a lorry or accidentally take out another member of the team. At this point, we reached a town called 'Arten'. Tom called to me and said, 'Look Ben! It's our turn; it's our turn! This is it, Ben!' I was fighting a personal battle with my own body but in that moment it hit home that this was a small part of a much bigger battle, being fought across the globe against slavery and exploitation. It's the turn of our generation to say 'no more'. The fight is urgent, we cannot just leave it to others – it's our turn to end it. To end slavery in all its grotesque forms.

* * * * *

If we wind back a few years, you will find me helping out backstage at an anti-trafficking awareness event. I knew nothing really about the modern slave trade and it was a real eye-opener. When I heard that slavery was going on now, despite the fact that it was abolished over 200 years ago, I was horrified. My first thought was about my two wonderful daughters; my youngest was just three at the time and I thought, if someone did that to her, I'd do something. I'd rip the world apart to free her.

My second thought was – it is someone's daughter. I should do something. So, naturally, as any young, passionate man would do, I booked the NEC arena and organized a huge anti-trafficking event for about 5,000 people called 'The Stand'. By some miracle it was a great success, thanks to the help and support of some wise friends, including Rob and Marion White. They went on to help me found the charity Hope for Justice following this event. When I look back over the last 5 years it is amazing to see how far we have come. From having just two staff members working out of a basement, we now have multi-disciplinary teams who are rescuing people every week.

It's been a steep learning curve, but I've always believed in being strategic and not just diving in without a plan. We now have a strategy which really seems to be working. Following our experiences in the first couple of years we came up with the idea of opening Regional Investigative Hubs in each area of the UK. We recognized the importance of local relationships and resources and so we want to put teams of experienced investigators all over the UK. We opened our first hub early in 2013 and named it Emma's Hub – to honor the first girl we rescued.

We were very fortunate in recruiting some top quality, experienced ex-police officers and the first hub has been a great success. In 2013 we assisted 104 victims of trafficking. An area that we have really developed is the training of local police and non-governmental organizations on spotting the signs of trafficking and how to deal with it. This empowers others to go and help more victims which grows the movement further than Hope for Justice.

We established our second hub early this year and have now merged with two other organizations in the US and Cambodia so that we are working internationally. I honestly believe that this system of investigation, rescue, aftercare, legal advice and training can bring an end to slavery in our nation.

* * * * *

One of the most important things to me is that the movement of Hope for Justice outgrows me. I don't want this to be the Ben Cooley anti-trafficking organization – as with William Wilberforce, I want the movement to outgrow the man, to inspire a whole generation to rise up against the injustice of slavery. I can start this charity and push it forward and do everything I can do to grow and develop it, but if it collapses after I'm gone then I have not achieved what I set out to do.

There have been some brilliant moments when I've been able to see this happen. A few years after Hope for Justice started we realized that we needed someone with a strong aftercare background, and so I embarked on searching for the right person. I interviewed this girl, Kate, and I didn't think I'd been that harsh, but later I was told that I absolutely tore her to shreds! She hadn't yet been here very long and had kept pretty quiet around me so far. Then one day we got a report in about a family who had been trafficked.

I didn't often attend rescues at this point, because we now had a team of experienced staff who were able to deal with it; however, because the family was quite large I pitched in to help. Kate met us outside the building and did a little debrief, but nothing prepared me for what I saw and experienced. I walked into this relatively large room and was hit by the smell of poverty. I've been out to places like India and Brazil and been into slums and places of extreme poverty, but I had never smelt this smell in England before. It was the smell of exploitation; it's horrendous, it goes beyond the smell of just being unwashed, it was the smell of abuse. I looked round and saw this family, and saw children, of a similar age to my own, sat with their backs to the wall and their heads in between their knees. Not for minutes, but for hours.

I offered my help and support and got told quite sharply by Kate to go out and get food – so I went off to the supermarket. There's that rule people say – don't go shopping when you're hungry. I also found that you should never go shopping when you've just seen an exploited family, because you try to buy the whole shop! I was walking around with full trolleys, and having seen the youngest child, just a baby, in that condition, I was throwing in baby stuff for 3 months to 3 years! After about an hour and a half of shopping I finally got back and gave everything out. Kate, who had been quite sheepish and shy in her interview, was suddenly now in the action and she turned round to me and barked, 'Where's the hot food?!'

I was meant to get hot food?! So out I go again and get the hot food and for some bizarre reason nowhere accepted card payments so it took me ages to get it. By the time I got back Kate was fuming that I'd been so long and part of me is thinking, 'Oh my gosh, I'm the CEO, leave me alone!' I put the hot food on the table and Kate ordered me to leave because there were too many of us and we were overwhelming the family. Despite feeling rather surprised and indignant, I smiled to myself as I left the room – I'd made the right decision taking her on!

Before I left, I noticed that for some reason the family didn't come up and eat any of the food I put on the table. Outside later, I asked Kate why they weren't eating. She told me that every night this family would sit on the floor around the table while the trafficker and his family would eat. When they had finished they would throw the scraps on the floor to the children. There wasn't enough for the mother, so she was malnourished and so was the baby. I realized in that moment that restoration is a long haul. They had been trained that food, and freedom, wasn't their right. So it was going to take a while for them to realize that they had a place at the table. A few weeks later our team went back to visit and the baby had big chubby cheeks and the children were running around and dancing – no longer sat with their backs against the wall. They had also made us a cake to say thank you for giving them their family and their freedom back.

* * * * *

Of course, my faith has been a powerful motivation for starting Hope for Justice. There are children as young as three being sold in the UK for the purposes of sexual exploitation, and I know that God wants me to do everything I can to stop this happening. The support I have had from the Church has been incredible, and I truly believe in the power of the local church to make an impact on this issue.

I want a generation to rise up that takes the gospel seriously – that does more than just talk, more than just speak on a platform. We are taught that faith without deeds is dead. People who have been trafficked are real human beings, with real lives, and that demands we demonstrate a real God who really helps them. We can be too safe in this country; sometimes if we really want to serve our purpose we need to take risks. We were born to serve the poor, the weak and the marginalized.

Human trafficking is a great and oppressive giant. But it's my firm belief that when ordinary people get involved, things change. You can see that when you look down through history. People like William Wilberforce, Martin Luther King, and Rosa Parks – whose simple refusal to give up her seat on a bus became a great symbol of the civil rights movement. There is a brilliant quote by Robert Kennedy:

> First is the danger of futility; the belief there is nothing one man or one woman can do against the enormous array of the world's ails – against misery, against ignorance, or injustice and violence . . . Few will have the greatness to bend history, but each of us can work to change a small portion of the events and in the total of all those acts will be written the history of this generation.

It is in our normalness, in a collective of small actions joined together, that begins a movement and makes a real impact on injustice and changes our society. Those small acts – signing up to give £5 a month, joining a campaigning group, writing to your MP – the combined individual acts of many is what will end slavery.

I've learnt that one man plus the power of God equals victory every time no matter what the odds. This means that when the Church gets involved in the darkest places, we can transform them. No matter how large the statistics, how dangerous the perpetrator, our God is able to use you and me to take down the biggest giants. A lot of people we meet want to dive in and start rescuing people straight away in any way they can, and I love the passion that this shows. However, I have also learnt the vital importance of having the right experience and qualifications for what is a very sensitive area of work with very vulnerable people. We need skilled social workers and investigators to make sure that we are doing the best we can for the people we help.

This doesn't mean that everyone else's skills are irrelevant. By just lending your voice and spreading the word, sacrificing some finances, or sacrificing time through volunteering and fundraising –

this can mean the difference between freedom and slavery. You don't have to go all out and give up everything in your life to make a difference; the small acts of a collective of individuals joined in the same cause are what change the world.

The Church is instrumental in our work. However, I also love that this issue stretches beyond and outside the walls of the Church – this is not just a 'Christian' issue, it is a human issue. This is a cause that we can all agree on and get behind, together – there are few who would deny that the end of slavery is a worthwhile goal, whatever their beliefs.

* * * * *

Even though I am still as passionate about ending slavery as I was when I first started, the last six years have not been an easy road. The hardest thing about starting Hope for Justice has been the fact that it takes all of you. It consumes you. It's affected every part of my life. People look at those who lead organizations and they think 'wow, wouldn't it be awesome, standing on a platform and speaking in front of thousands of people', or 'wouldn't it be awesome to meet this person, to have the privilege of going into 10 Downing Street and speaking in Parliament' – but people don't see the other part. Where you start in a basement and you get rejection after rejection after rejection; where you are told you're a nobody and that you shouldn't start because you won't make any difference anyway. For me the hardest part is the rejection. The hardest part is the personal cost of people not believing in you.

I used to be part of the leadership teams of a couple of different organizations and I was always the one in the room saying that we can do bigger, we can do better. But when, in reality, it's down to you, you're the one who has to make all the final decisions – that's a different level of responsibility, a different sense of leadership, and it can really take its toll. The fact that it's been down to me, and that if we had failed it would have been on my shoulders – that's the hard part. And that's where faith steps in. That I'm not doing this alone and, however much it may sometimes feel like it, it's not all on my shoulders. There's a bigger plan in place and God is steering us in the right direction.

I've learnt in the last six years that there is a lot of darkness and oppression in the world; that there are a lot of things wrong. But at the same time, the most important thing I have discovered is that there is also a lot of good. When starting off fighting something called slavery you can get very cynical, negative and critical about the world, but I have realized that there is an army of good people. There is a whole mass of good in this world that needs to be celebrated. I've learnt the ability to celebrate the good and focus on changing the bad, without losing something called joy. I believe that enjoying this process of changing the world, enjoying being with fellow world changers, enjoying the fact that we get to change lives and change systems for the better so that they protect the poor and the marginalized, enjoying the fact that we get to change the system so that violence and oppression is not tolerated: this is one of the greatest things that you can do with your life. To enjoy changing the world, rather than endure it. I believe that being part of an organization like this is not to be endured but enjoyed and we do – we have fun along the way. That is what Hope for Justice is: people who see the hope they can bring with their life and with their resolve; people who see that with determination they can begin to see transformation and change. We believe that freedom is worth the fight. If you agree, join the movement to end slavery!

Hope for Justice identifies and rescues victims of human trafficking, advocates on their behalf, provides restorative care which rebuilds lives and trains frontline professionals to tackle slavery. From five offices across three continents, Hope for Justice operates a proven multi-disciplinary model based on years of combined experience. Ben Cooley, CEO, heads their growing team of professionals who are pioneering programs to bring freedom, restoration and justice to modern day slaves throughout the world.

http://hopeforjustice.org/

Chapter 7
A Change of Perspective
Peter Stanley

Our senses were assaulted by the sights and smells of Mumbai as my friend and I rode a cab to the rendezvous point where we would meet our pimp. Even at night the heat was oppressive and vehicles jostled one another down crowded streets in the frenetic traffic. Taxis, cycles and cars raced five abreast under streetlights, avoiding potholes and stray animals, narrowly avoiding accidents at every turn.

Riding alongside the driver was our contact. He had set up the meeting and would be joining us on this excursion. Once we met with our pimp, he would then lead us to the brothel we had agreed to visit. Our cover story was that we were sex tourists from England, looking for 'fresh young girls.' The job of the man we were to meet was to take people just like us to the brothels where he acted as a feeder.

We arrived at the designated street corner and sure enough he was waiting. He slipped into the car quickly and instructed the driver. We set off again into the night.

Questions raced through my mind. How exactly does one look and act like a sex tourist? I had no idea. I hoped that our pimp wouldn't ask any awkward questions and smell a rat. Fortunately, he spent most of the time talking to our contact. We just sat quietly in the back, feeling extraordinarily anxious.

What were we doing here? The purpose of our trip to India was to help a team of anti-trafficking investigators pinpoint the illegal use of minors. In India prostitution isn't illegal, but using minors for sex is. Ben Cooley and I were helping the Oasis team to track down victims who had likely been trafficked to Mumbai and were trapped here in brothels.

We had been warned that the brothels were dangerous places. Pimps carry firearms with them in case of trouble. Punters are usually locked in while using the brothel.

It has been known for undercover investigators to be beaten up or forced to follow through with girls if their cover is blown. All of this put into perspective our valiant efforts to help the victims – they seemed a step too far. Back at the hotel our wives were as nervous as we were, with the unenviable task of waiting, not knowing what was happening.

Earlier that evening our contact had assured us that a back-up team would be following us at a safe distance in another car – ready to come to our rescue, should anything go wrong. However, that plan quickly unraveled once our pimp got in the car. He switched our intended destination.

We would not be visiting the brothel we thought, but another one, located elsewhere across town. The first brothel had been raided the night before; the plan had changed. Sitting in the back, the two of us had no idea our back-up team had lost us and our contact had no way of giving them the new address. It was best we didn't know. We journeyed on in ignorance.

After an hour we pulled into a derelict-looking side street. It was populated with potholes, broken streetlights, the backs of hotels with rubbish piled high, and stank of urine. The pimp ushered us towards the street corner and told us to await the signal to move forward. The local police were currently in the brothel, taking their weekly bribe. It would be inappropriate to enter at the same time. So we waited.

It's funny how we can experience a sense of peace, even amongst chaos and danger. That's what was going through my mind as I stood there, full of nerves. I remembered that friends in England had promised to pray for our safety, so I texted them to pray at that moment. Instantly a reply came back: they were praying. It heartened me no end.

Then, strangely and wonderfully, I caught the strains of music drifting out of a nearby window. It was a Christian worship song I knew and loved. This was the best reassurance I could have wished for.

A figure exited the steel-shuttered building next to us. We were given our cue to walk down the street. Again, I wondered how a sex tourist would feel and look, but had no point of reference. I just trusted we'd do this right.

The place was small with three rooms downstairs and the same upstairs. We were led through the steel door and invited to sit down in a waiting room. The scene was one of the most surreal I have ever encountered. A normal sized lounge; a single sofa and chair; a water cooler; a cheap TV showing some local chat show. It was a picture of domesticity. The pimp, our contact and the two of us sat down and waited.

In due course a short, fat lady aged around 60 came in. She looked like any typical grandma or aunty. She greeted us and offered us a glass of water, telling us the girls were coming down soon.

My mind struggled to comprehend how this nice little old lady could be the madam of a brothel, which could be dealing in young children for sexual exploitation by sex tourists. There were no horns, no sinister looks, just a pleasant woman whom I might chat to over a garden fence.

As we waited, I wondered what I would say to get myself out of having to go upstairs with a girl. I knew our contact had been put in danger by refusing before. I had no answer. I chose to trust our contact and prayed under my breath.

Minutes went by until 'Angelica' and another girl came down to show themselves to us. Under the glare of the lounge lights they stood a few feet away from us and waited. I had assumed there would be some attempt at sexually alluring makeup and clothes, but there was none of this. They looked Russian, in their late twenties, wore jeans and T-shirts and looked really quite bored. No attempt had been made to dress up.

The girls gave a 'Here we go again' glance at each other. The madam apologized to us, and said that because of a religious festival, there had been a rush on local young girls and these were all she could offer. To our enormous relief, we had been given our excuse.

Both of us joined with our contact in saying how disappointed we were not to have 'fresh young girls.' These girls weren't what we were after. The madam apologized again and promised better girls the next night if we wanted. We agreed and got up to walk out.

The conversation had been conducted right in front of Angelica and her friend. They simply stood there like objects – no basic human dignity afforded them. They turned and walked back upstairs as we made our way out past the guard and into the side street.

Relief flooded through us as we walked away. We began to speak but were hastily silenced. 'Be quiet and don't speak until we are in a taxi,' our contact cautioned. 'We're being followed.' It wasn't until we drove away that we could believe this ordeal had ended.

In the event, we hadn't located any minors, but we had helped our contact and his anti-trafficking agency gain valuable information, plus an invitation for him to return in due course. Only when we re-joined the team did we learn that we had conducted the whole operation without support. But the words of the worship song still echoed around my head as a reminder that we had not been forgotten.

Exploits like these make for interesting stories, but some people do this for a job. Our contact was a church pastor who had hung up his robes in order to join a team of investigators to fight for what he believed to be right. Nightly he would leave his home and his wife would stay behind, praying that he came home safely in the morning.

So how did I come to be investigating brothels in downtown Mumbai?

My journey

I was no great social crusader. In fact, I can be quite selfish and would often turn my back on charity appeals that came through the door or appeared on TV.

I had worked in London as an insurance underwriter for many years, doing deals and taking risks with my companies' funds. I worked to raise a family and pay the mortgage, enjoying the cut and thrust of international risk management. It was all a world away from the anti-trafficking battle in India.

For me, it took several steps to move away from what I was doing. It began ten years ago with a meeting with a careers adviser when I realized that though I enjoyed my work, I became animated about the subject of humanitarian work. The conversation planted a seed that meant, when the circumstances were right, I would make the switch.

A short while later, I did. Since then I have worked as project manager and strategic adviser to South London community projects and anti-trafficking organizations in England, Holland and India. I have set up three new organizations and continue to offer advice to others who ask. It has been a total change of scenery from the world of London underwriting. Two things took me there:

First, I saw that my skills in project management and strategy were easily transferable to any sphere of work, from finance to media, to humanitarian work and so on. Second, my Christian faith was drawing me to become more involved in supporting those in need.

I would hasten to add that it is not wrong to simply earn a living to support your family. We each have a call on our lives and must follow our own paths. But for me, it led to anti-trafficking and other social enterprises.

Once I made my mind to leave the City of London, I knew it was the right step. My salary dropped dramatically, but it was what I wanted to do. During my farewell drinks in a City wine bar, I was told by numerous fellow underwriters that they envied me for doing what I clearly wanted to do. Many felt trapped by mortgages, other financial commitments and, above all, the fear of change.

Chance meeting

It's funny how life can suddenly change based on an apparent chance encounter. Those of us who have a faith believe that God has a hand in such situations. For me, becoming involved in anti-human trafficking was one such occasion. I had heard about the possibility of modern slavery, like most people, but that was the extent of my knowledge. All that changed at a wedding reception in a converted barn in Surrey.

For the previous seven years I had worked on a Croydon community project. As that time drew to a close, I felt God wanted me to take some time out and wait for the next chapter of my life to unfold – it was going to be quite a change. It was a beautiful summer, so the prospect of relaxing in the garden while I contemplated my future was no hardship.

Then my friend, Martin Richards, called me with an interesting message: 'I had a dream that a train was coming and that you had to get on it. It appeared that this was a picture of your next stage in life. You had to prepare to get on the train and not miss it.'

I thanked my friend and mused on this picture. I had received similar messages before and they often foretold something. When things like this happen we tend to store them away on a mental shelf and wait to see what happens.

Just a few days later another friend, Dan Jackson from Alabama, USA, emailed me. He too had received a 'picture' that he knew was for me. A train was coming; I had to prepare to board it, otherwise I was in danger of missing it. Receiving two such similar messages in close proximity got my attention, and the next five months were a time of anticipation. By late September, both my wife and I felt that something was about to happen and it would probably begin in October.

Our friend's wedding took place on the last day of September. At the reception in the barn we were chatting to Steve Chalke of the charity Oasis, catching up on news. I told him I was preparing to volunteer for a good cause for three months before I got stuck into some new ventures. I asked him to keep this in the back of his mind in case he came across something that might suit me.

'Back of my mind?' he said. 'It's at the front of my mind! I know exactly what you can do. We and a number of other organizations have started to plan a short-term awareness campaign about human trafficking. When can you start?'

I had booked a two-week holiday to St Lucia that began the next day, but Steve insisted on emailing me some details to look over. So the following week I lay on a sun lounger reading about human trafficking. It was ironic that my introduction to the world of trafficking began where so much of it had taken place two centuries earlier. Suffice to say, I agreed to volunteer part-time for three months as Strategy Director in order to see the 'Stop the Traffik' campaign completed.

Those next three months, Bex Keer and I shared a small office with a white board, two desks and a lot of questions. We asked ourselves how best to get the message out. But what was the message?

Most of the public had little understanding of 'people trafficking.' I regularly faced confused looks as I explained it to people and they tried to picture how a transport issue could be linked to slavery. It seems strange that only ten years ago the phrase was so new to us all. Now, it has become a common term.

We wondered how we could generate public interest in the subject. We had good links with a number of conferences that some of us spoke at, but we needed to create a message to reach the public at large.

I asked a friend of mine if there was any chance an advertising agency could help us. I told him we had no money and would ask for a 'pro bono' account. A few weeks later, I had three large London advertising agencies all pitching for our business, competing to provide Stop the Traffik with free advertising expertise.

Leagus Delaney won the deal and quickly started to help us see that human trafficking, at its core, was simply treating people as commodities – buying and selling them like groceries, not valuing them as people. Together, with a small team of web designers called Contrapositive, we worked on a number of films, posters and activities based on the strap line, 'People Should Not Be Bought and Sold.'

It was a strong message and as a result large numbers of similar organizations joined our loosely organized coalition. The public, too, signed up to local activism and the campaign took off. After the three months, this short-term campaign to mark the bicentenary of the abolition of the slave trade in the British Empire was far from over. The forming partner agencies agreed that Stop the Traffik should become a long-term initiative.

Since that small start in Lambeth, Stop the Traffik has gathered more than a thousand coalition members in over a hundred countries. Its team have written speeches for members of the House of Lords, been appointed special advisers to the UN, run awareness-raising concerts with rock bands and signed up thousands of students and church groups to local action projects. After I left, Ruth Dearnley took over, and she and her team have built on the groundswell, locally and internationally.

The missing ingredient

Yet, in those first exciting months, there still seemed to me to be one thing missing. Every successful campaign must have a message that really engages people where they are – to go beyond 'Oh dear, that's terrible,' to 'I need to do something about this, because it affects me.' Then it happened.

I had been talking with a colleague, Phil Lane, in Belgium, about the effect of slavery on everyday life and about the consumer products that have slavery in their supply chains. If we could find one or two, maybe we could show people that they were directly buying slave-contaminated products. Then they were affected whether they liked it or not. We talked about cotton, cheap clothes from sweat shops, chocolate and copper for mobile phones.

As I commuted into London one day, I vividly imagined a Sun newspaper story exposing slavery in the chocolate industry with a picture of a well-known chocolate bar on the front cover. The rest is history.

Stop the Traffik has spent years motivating community groups in many countries to campaign for 'slave-free chocolate.' Members of the team have become leading lobbyists for this issue, a thorn in the side of most of the big cocoa conglomerates. Now we have Fair Trade chocolate in our shops and human trafficking has been adopted as a popular cause for the long term.

Exciting and rewarding as all this was, I sometimes asked myself, 'Am I doing this for a job, or is it a heart-felt cause for me?' If it was the former, I might as well campaign for the price of turnips, for all the good it would do me personally.

I was keen that my faith should be a major motivator for what I was doing and that I hadn't just swapped conversations about insurance for those about people trafficking. I felt convicted that my Christian morals should be the driver for what I did. Two things happened at that time to truly make that change. One was my trip to Mumbai, to experience human trafficking at first hand. The other was a film premiere.

Lionsgate Films had asked Stop the Traffik to publicize the film Amazing Grace, and help build a groundswell of interest ... and box office! At the premiere, I spoke to the lead actors and heard myself say to Benedict Cumberbatch, 'I am a modern-day William Wilberforce.' The words came out with such force and conviction that they took me by surprise. I knew I had discovered something about myself that I had not previously understood. Here was my motivation.

According to the story line, William Wilberforce started his thirty-year crusade against slavery in a field next to his house, when he felt God ask him to carry out a specific 'work.' In his journal of 1787 he wrote, 'God Almighty has set before me two great objects, the suppression of the Slave Trade and the Reformation of Manners (Moral Values).'

From that moment on, I knew that I had a calling – albeit set in the 21st Century, so it would look completely different to Wilberforce. It is important to know our motivation for any good work. It acts as the core motivator when times are tough and inspiration dries up.

Close to home

I live in Croydon. It is a bustling London borough with a business center, several shopping malls and around 350,000 residents. It has been home to my family for over twenty years and we know it well – the shops, the schools, the parks. We feel at home here.

Central London is a twenty-minute train ride away. We all know that if human trafficking is occurring, it's up there – amongst the strip clubs, dubious looking business fronts and street begging. It is in the big cities, not the leafy suburbs, where all the problems are ... right?

One day I picked up the local newspaper and the headline shocked me to the point of disbelief. The police had just raided two houses *in my street* and discovered cannabis factories along with imprisoned young boys, suspected of being trafficked. Here I was talking to audiences around the world about human trafficking being in every community, yet I had not seen it on my own doorstep. I had walked past these houses on numerous occasions, never suspecting anything.

I began to follow the progress of the Croydon Community Against Trafficking, who pioneered mapping of possible human trafficking organizations in the town. Using trained volunteers they monitored signs of suspicious brothels and escort agencies and found over one hundred illegal locations in their own community.

The fact is, signs of slavery exist all around us. I run a mentoring agency called Ment4, that counsels troubled and vulnerable youth. Recently, one of the girls we were mentoring ran away from home. She was eventually found living in a house where she was being given 'free' drugs. Then she was being coerced into sleeping with the man's friends for money. She was probably being groomed for continued future sexual exploitation.

Again, this was happening in my home town. We all need to be aware that we could be walking past slavery happening without realizing it – unless we keep our eyes open. Make no mistake: it is happening on your doorstep as well as mine.

The fight against slavery

Over the last few years I have worked with the UK Human Trafficking Centre, as well as an Indian detection and aftercare agency, faith groups specializing in seeking justice, and with a victim of trafficking who set up her own charity to help survivors like herself. In working with such organizations in the voluntary sector and also with government, I have been heartened and also saddened by different attitudes.

On the positive side, the response from youth organizations has been fantastic. One university signed up freshers to their anti-human trafficking group with just as much success as the James Bond Society.

Young people have always been the most receptive to the message and they have taken on the cause in huge numbers. Perhaps it is because it is people their age who are being sold into slavery, so they readily identify with them. Young people need a good cause to fight for and many have adopted the fight against slavery as theirs.

The other group that has embraced the cause has been the church. Up and down the country I have seen congregations stir themselves to start action groups, to boycott non-Fair Trade chocolate and to publicize the issues.

On my travels talking to groups, a number of church ministers told me that they had previously fought a losing battle to stir their people to social concern and action. For years they had tried to engage them in good causes and failed. But slavery opened the door. It was this one topic that led people to a greater consciousness of social evils and provided the motivation for them to do something about it.

Then there are the negatives, the disappointing aspects of the fight against slavery that can be seen in meetings with government, police and particularly voluntary sector groups. We were all fighting a common enemy, yet I didn't see the degree of cooperation I hoped for, particularly amongst awareness and lobbying organizations.

There was an all-too-common spirit of competition and mistrust. Meetings would end in friction, point-scoring and squabbling. The underlying reason was easy to see: a competing struggle for grant-funding income. The higher the profile of an organization, the more likely they were to receive funding.

I have considered this issue of division from a faith perspective too. For those of us for whom faith is real, there is a bigger picture than that which is occurring in front of our eyes. Slavery is a dark trade with evil spiritual roots. Is it any surprise that those same dark forces war to divide and undermine those trying to dismantle them?

Slavery is an evil fuelled by greed, division and oppression. It operates by isolating people from their families and communities. It then imposes oppression on a person so thoroughly that it breaks their spirit. I don't believe this is possible without the contributing factor of evil spiritual forces.

So, for those working in the fight against slavery, apart from the common rivalries, there is also the risk of spiritual oppression – a factor which has led many to feeling overwhelmed and close to giving up. It is a naïve person who confronts such a powerful force without understanding that they need to protect themselves from counter attacks. Some might dismiss this as superstitious nonsense, but I have no reason to doubt that it is a very real aspect of modern slavery.

The question of faith

This is why I personally believe that the dimension of faith is so important in bringing change. History also shows us that Christian faith was operating at the heart of many of the great social reforms of our time. However, I don't believe that it is only people of faith who can combat the evils of society. Motivation is important, but to be successful in eradicating slavery we must remain focused on the most important people – the victims.

I have often been asked about my faith and whether the organizations I've worked with are 'Christian' ones. For my answer,

I take my cue from my colleague, Nick Kinsella, at the UK Human Trafficking Centre, who says that everything they do must be 'victim centered.' This keeps the focus on humanity and the alleviation and prevention of suffering. Any campaign or legal action based purely based on numbers and statistics will quickly become heartless.

So my reply has always been that the focus is on the victim, regardless of race, color or creed. There is no bias. My faith acts as my personal motivator for doing good – we all need a motivator to achieve great things in life. For me, the Christian faith, with its belief in the value of human life and redemption, can motivate and sustain me through difficult times.

What can we do?

Today I look back on a decade of learning about and working for a cause far greater than my personal world. I was a businessman who had little regard for the suffering of others and had barely heard of human trafficking. My heart now is softer through experiencing first-hand the pain of victims and reading the countless stories of others. But my belief in a breakthrough in conquering the slave trade grows and my faith leads me to believe in a greater force for good. I am glad to be a part of it.

For those impacted by the stories of people of faith who have fought a similar fight; for those who want to join in, but don't know how – start where you are and do what you can. Everyone can help, whether doing something small or large.

In Amsterdam there is a great little café run by Youth With A Mission. It is sandwiched between the Central Station and the red light district and serves excellent mint tea, if you like that kind of thing. On one occasion I was down in the basement with a colleague, talking with a small group of interested young people about our cause, encouraging them to join in. Many of them did.

For one in particular, Antonie Fountain, it changed his life. He gave up his marketing job, corporate salary and company car to start a

Dutch branch of our organization. He had a no office, no salary and no idea where this would take him, but he and his wife, Jerinke, had faith to take him where his heart wanted to go.

Several years later he is a leading international lobbyist in the cocoa industry, speaking about human trafficking in the chocolate supply chain. He speaks to the UN, media networks and parliamentarians. How interesting to see how a small spark in the right place can start something quite significant.

Equally, it is easy to sign up to organizations like Love 146, the Salvation Army, Stop the Traffik, Hope for Justice, and to donate to them. It is easy to join a voluntary action group and give a few hours a week to a good cause. For those with a Christian faith, I encourage you to pray and ask God to direct you and touch your heart. Who knows where it may take you. I certainly had no clue those ten years ago.

Peter Stanley left a well-established career in the City of London's financial district to pursue the call of God into humanitarian work. His first role was as Strategy Director for the international campaign Stop the Traffik, *which he helped develop into a global movement of individuals, communities and organizations that are working to prevent human trafficking around the world. Peter is now a consultant to many diverse groups combatting modern slavery and recently founded a mentoring agency for troubled teenagers, which he runs in his home town of Croydon, Greater London.*

Chapter 8
Let the Slaves Speak
Baroness Caroline Cox

Speak up for those who cannot speak for themselves.
For the rights of all who are destitute. Speak up and judge fairly;
Defend the rights of the poor and needy.
(Proverbs 31: 8-9, NIV)

As Christians, we have a biblical obligation to speak for those who
have been denied a voice, to protect and promote the rights of the
destitute, the poor and the needy, and to speak out against injustice.

None are more in need of this ministry than slaves, who are
denied all rights and an independent voice, often subjected to
abuse of every kind and forced to live in destitution, humiliation
and dehumanizing dependence on another person with complete
power them.

William Wilberforce's Christian faith – combined with a meeting
with the dedicated slavery abolitionist Thomas Clarkson on Sunday
October 28, 1787 – led him to write in his diary: 'God Almighty has
set before me two great objects, the suppression of the slave trade
and the reformation of society.' From 1788, he fought resolutely for
the abolition of the slave trade, but faced such fierce opposition that

it was not until 22nd February 1807 that the House of Commons eventually voted overwhelmingly for the abolition of the slave trade in the British Empire.

Political battles and subsequent achievements continued until, in August 1833, the British Parliament took the final step of the abolition of slavery throughout the Empire: 700,000 people still held as slaves were freed with a decree that their masters would be given £20 million in compensation.

Wilberforce had devoted 53 years to this long and arduous battle for the emancipation of slaves, which finally resulted in success just three days before he died. He responded with these joyful words: 'Thank God that I've lived to witness the day in which England is willing to give 20 million pounds sterling for the abolition of slavery.'

William Wilberforce was able to die knowing that his hard-fought endeavors, inspired and strengthened by his Christian faith, had achieved a momentous success that resulted in the freeing of hundreds of thousands of people from the bondage of slavery.

In 2007, we celebrated the bicentenary of William Wilberforce's first hard-won parliamentary achievement: the abolition of the slave trade in the British Empire. But I feared this would encourage the belief that slavery is a horror of the past. Instead, this barbaric, dehumanizing practice has shifted into a less visible form – which makes it even harder to measure and combat.

In 2007, it was estimated that there were at least 27 million men, women and children suffering some form of slavery; since then, there has been not only a continuation, but a possible expansion, ranging from the deeply alarming increase in human trafficking on our own doorsteps, to the ideologically motivated abduction and enslavement practiced by burgeoning Islamist terrorist groups such as Boko Haram in West Africa and Islamic State militants in the Middle East.

Therefore, William Wilberforce's mission is far from accomplished. He fulfilled his duty courageously and tenaciously in his own day.

What are we doing to play our part in endeavors to abolish this vile practice from the face of the earth in our day? Those of us who are Christians have an unequivocal, compelling moral imperative to obey the Biblical mandate to alleviate the suffering of the oppressed and to challenge injustice.

Many people may not know that slavery still exists, but there is abundant evidence. Therefore, I hope that this book will raise awareness and provide the evidence so that the horrific reality of modern slavery will disturb and challenge us all to do everything we can to eradicate it. Anyone who reads the evidence will no longer be able to claim ignorance as an excuse for inaction.

However, although the statistics are deeply shocking, they cannot portray the human anguish of slavery as it affects an individual person and his or her family and community. Therefore, in this chapter I will tell the real-life stories of people into whose eyes I have looked, who have endured the horrors of enslavement – and their voices speak for those whose voices we cannot hear because they are still enslaved.

We will hear authentic stories from victims of different forms of contemporary slavery, and each of those stories could be multiplied by countless more.[1]

1. Slavery as a weapon of war, ideologically justified.

Sudan suffered a horrendous war from 1989 until 2005 when a Comprehensive Peace Agreement was signed, with provision for South Sudan to achieve independence. During that war, 2 million died; 4 million people were displaced and hundreds of thousands of men, women and children were abducted into slavery.

---

1. This chapter includes material published in This Immoral Trade: Slavery in the 21st Century, Baroness Caroline Cox and others, Monarch Books, 2013. This book also contains many more real-life stories.

The war still continues in Darfur, South Kordofan and Blue Nile with ruthless policies of ethnic and religious cleansing inflicted by the government of Sudan under President Al-Bashir, who has been indicted by the International Criminal Court.

I visited the war-afflicted areas many times, often to help to rescue slaves. On those visits, we were repeatedly told by local leaders and some of the Arabs from the north who helped with the rescue operations, that the ideological justification for enslavement was the forced Arabisation of Africans and Islamisation of non-Muslims to achieve Al-Bashir's vision of a unified Arabic, Islamic State.

I was able to participate in the rescue of many hundreds of women and children from slavery. Each person told a heart-wrenching story of abuse, terror, maltreatment, humiliation and extreme physical and mental suffering. Two of these rescued slaves must speak for all the rest – including the thousands who are still missing today.

Bol Deng, a 52-year old man[2] described his experiences:

> I was at the market in Abin Dau with my five children (ranging in age from 16 to 3 years old) when the raiders came. We were all taken captive. I was tied by my wrists in a chain to other captives. The journey to the North was very hard. We had to walk for about two solid days. We were given scarcely any food and I, and my children, were beaten. I have a scar on my wrist from where I was bound.
>
> At the end of my journey I was separated from my family and taken to a camp in Shetep, where I was held for three months. There were approximately 400 men in the camp. My hands and my legs were tied. Those who ran the camp put constant pressure on me to convert to Islam. About twice a day they would tell me that I should

---

2. Names in stories of slaves this story have been changed to protect the anonymity of the persons involved.

convert. They told me that we should all become Muslim and then it would be possible to live together as brothers but that if we did not they would kill us all . . .

On several occasions this was accompanied by beatings. About a week after my arrival I was beaten severely with sticks. The upper bone in my arm now sticks out as a result of this beating. On another occasion, during the night, they came to me again and told me that I must become a Muslim and that they would beat me if I did not.

I am a Christian and have committed myself to Christ. I cannot change my belief. As I would not comply with their commands, they attacked me, stamping on my chest. I was nearly paralyzed. After five days I still could not stand up or use my legs or my hands properly. I have a visible scar on my chest from that attack. I am still suffering with pain in my back, along my spine and in my chest and my hips.

There are people . . . who are not against us but are sympathetic to us. They came and talked to me and told me that everyone is born to be free. They paid money for me and brought me back to the South. I am so happy to be back here . . . My greatest difficulty is that my whole body is in pain. Also, my wife and my five children are still in the North. However, seeing you here gladdens my heart. Those who secured my freedom are like the *hand of God reaching out to save me.*

Abuk , a woman about 34 years old:

In May 1998 Sudanese Popular Defence Forces, together with Murahaleen [the armed militia] came on horseback and attacked my village, Aweng (Bahr-El Ghazal). They killed many people, mainly men, including my brother and my nephew. Some of those killed were fighting the forces but many were unarmed civilians.

I was taken captive with two of my three children and a large number of other women and children. My captors snatched my two-year-old son, Mayai, from me and threw him harshly on the ground. He still has a scar on his chest from where he was hurt as he was thrown down on to a sharp object.

Our wrists were tied and we were tied to horses. The children were placed on the horses and we were forced to walk for 10 days to the north. We were told that all the people in the village would be killed. We were given very little sustenance, just dura [sorghum] mixed with sand, and water which had been polluted with urine. This was deliberately done to show the raiders' contempt for us. One of the children died on the way from hunger. I and the other women were sexually abused during the trip to the North.

I was taken to Kitep near Goth in Western Sudan where I was kept by the man who had captured me in the raid. His name is Feki and I lived with him and his wife, who both mistreated me. There were five of us who had been taken as slaves who were kept in his household. My children were taken away from me and given to someone else.

I was completely distraught; I did not know what to do; I did not know where my children were and I did not know whether my husband and my 5-year-old daughter, Ajak, who had not been taken North, were still alive. I felt overwhelmed and completely helpless.

2. Abduction of children and enforced recruitment as child soldiers

This practice has continued to modern times, in countries such as Burma with 70,000 child soldiers before recent reforms, and Uganda where the infamous rebel army led by Joseph Konya reportedly abducted at least 25,000 children, forcing them to fight with his Lord's Resistance Army (LRA) against their own people and against the Ugandan Army.

My small NGO HART (Humanitarian Aid Relief Trust) responded to appeals to provide help for the people in Pader District, northern Uganda, one of the most heavily afflicted areas in the epicenter of LRA activity. While there, we met many young people who had escaped from the LRA: their accounts of their ordeals were spine-chillingly consistent but each with its own particular horrors.

Richard, 22, from Wangduku West, was abducted March 5, 1999. He was sleeping in his hut, alone, as his mother had died and his brothers had left. He was taken with other abductees to Welle, about 15 km away, in single file (not tied up); he was beaten and made to carry a heavy load of fresh cassava. En route, the soldiers slaughtered a large goat and hung it around his neck. He was taken to Sudan (Rubanga Tek) where he was trained under Commander Otti. He excelled at his training and was very good at firing at targets in the tree.

His first active encounter was in Sudan in the an operation known as 'Iron Fist.' Then the LRA fled and he had to climb a very steep mountain where Kony, the notorious LRA leader, was stationed. Many abductees either slipped accidentally to their death or, if they foundered, the Commander shot them and they rolled to their death.

He returned to Uganda, where he was involved in much fighting and abduction in the Patongo locality. He didn't beat the abductees, but tied them up and escorted them. During this time, he claims he was forced to do 3 things: to rape a woman publicly; to kill another abductee with a hoe; and to throw an abductee down a well.

He received injuries from torture and on one occasion he was beaten repeatedly with a bicycle chain, after which he passed blood in his urine. The beating was punishment for taking too long to push the abductee down the well.

In one battle, he was shot in the leg and captured by the Ugandan Army, and taken to a Rehabilitation Centre in 2003. Whilst there, he learnt that the LRA killed his mother because he had escaped − she was beaten to death. His father had died before he had been abducted. He had one brother who had also been abducted but came under a different command; his brother was then transferred to his Unit, whereupon he arranged his escape.

He has two sisters, one unmarried, with a child. He feels there has been a big change in his life (since coming to the Rehabilitation Centre) because he is now loved.

Irene, 15, from Latwong, was abducted in 2001. The LRA came to the village, near Pajule and attacked for much of the night. She was abducted but neither tied nor beaten. She was made to carry the Commander's heavy bag.

During 19 months with the LRA, she was transferred to two different Commanders' Units. She didn't receive intensive training but during captivity she was made to kill, using three methods.

Abductees would be tied up and the neck cut with a panga knife; or the belly would be slashed open with a panga knife; or they would be beaten to death. She was warned that if she failed to comply they would cut her neck so that she would bleed to death, and they cut her neck superficially in two places (scars just visible).

She knows she killed 10 abductees (children and adults) by slashing the belly, scooping up the blood and placing it in her mouth. On another occasion, she was cooking for the Commander when the Ugandan Army came. She ran and left the food on the fire which burnt and as a consequence she was beaten unconscious.

She escaped early one morning when she went to collect water for the Commander's bath. She walked for one mile down the road and left the water container; she then ran through the bush and made her way towards home. She was picked up by the Ugandan Army, transferred to the police and then to the Rehabilitation Centre on June 3, 2003.

Talking about the killings, she explains how she had been indoctrinated to understand that if she did not kill the abductee, then the panga knife would be given over for the abductee to kill her. She felt it was wrong. She is now in school, but cannot concentrate and has repeated nightmares about the first killing which occurred at dawn and the first time she had to drink blood.

3. Sexual Slavery

The abduction of women and girls and their subjugation as sex slaves takes many forms and occurs in many countries. Three examples must speak for all:

- Devadasis or temple prostitutes in India
- Rape as a weapon of war in Burma
- Human trafficking in Europe

Devadasis, or temple prostitutes, are the victims of a centuries' old practice in parts of India. Usually associated with poverty-stricken families or mothers who are already Devadasis, the practice involves the dedication of a young girl to a temple for 'Temple Service.' The ceremony may involve a small celebration and the child is given a necklace of red and white beads.

At the time, some of the children are happy and proud of their beads, not realizing that they are symbols of condemnation to a nightmarish existence: on reaching puberty, they begin 'servicing' up to 20 men a day in some brothel-prison or being subjected to the role of the 'available woman' for a village, where they will be denied dignity and the opportunity to marry.

One woman said in anguish: *'I have had a thousand men in my life – but never a husband.'* These women not only have to endure the physical suffering and humiliation of enforced prostitution; they also suffer the anguish of giving birth to, and being responsible for illegitimate children, many of them with HIV, who will find it very hard to have any opportunity for education, marriage, or any other prerequisite for a reasonable quality of life.

Abduction, slavery and rape as a weapon of war

This centuries old vile practice has continued into our day and is being practiced in many countries. In some countries it is ideologically justified: the self-avowed Islamist terrorist group, Boko Haram, has been abducting and subjecting girls to sexual slavery as part of its policy of eliminating Christians from Northern Nigeria and putting into practice policies designed to eradicate Western education, especially for girls. There have also been reports of the abduction and subjection into sexual slavery of women and girls captured by Islamist militants in Iraq and Syria.

The abhorrent practice of rape as a weapon of war has been practiced in many other countries, including modern Burma, where there are numerous reports of the Burmese Army using rape as a weapon of war over many decades in Karen, Karenni and Mon States. At the time of writing, they are continuing to inflict this torture on girls and women in regions belonging to ethnic tribal peoples such as the predominantly Buddhist Shan, Muslim Rohingya and Christian Kachin peoples[3].

---

3. Pushed to the Brink by Kachin Women's Association Thailand, June 2013.

The following case study comes from a now deserted village which I visited during a HART visit to Kachin State:

Sumlut Roi Ja: The Supreme Court as a Tool to Maintain Impunity[4]

Sumlut Roi Ja is a 28-year-old mother who was arrested by Burma Army soldiers on October 28th 2011 while working on a family's farm near her village Hkai Bang, close to the China border. Her husband and father-in-law were also arrested and forced at gunpoint to carry corn to a military camp, Battalion 321, at Mubum. They managed to escape, but Sumlut Roi Ja was recaptured.

After her abduction, she was seen at the military camp by several witnesses. According to men who escaped from the outpost, she was being made to clean and cook for the soldiers during the day, and was gang-raped by them at night. A Kachin Women's Association Thailand (KWAT) documenter reported seeing Sumlut through a zoom lens from a nearby hilltop on October 31. The next day, on November 1, she was able to see a woman being dragged by four soldiers into a bunker at the camp, but could not clearly identify her. After that, she had not been able to see any women at the camp.

On November 1, Sumlut's family members met with Lt. Col. Zaw Myo Htut, the Burma Army commander at the Loi Je military base, and begged for her release. He told them that she would be released on November 2, but they waited the whole day at the foot of the mountain and she did not appear. It is now presumed that Sumlut Roi Ja has been killed.

In January 2012, a Kachin lawyer assisted Sumlut's husband to file a case at the Supreme Court at Naypyidaw

---

4. Same Impunity Same Patterns, Women's League of Burma, January 2014.

against Light Infantry Brigade (LIB) 321 for the abduction of his wife. He travelled to attend the hearing on February 23. However, he was not permitted to speak, although he had witnessed the abduction. The court simply heard the testimony of a lieutenant from LIB 321, who asserted that no woman by the name of Roi Ja had been detained at the camp.

On 23 February, 2012, the Naypyidaw Supreme Court dismissed the case for lack of evidence. The judge based his ruling entirely on the testimony of the military defendants. Falsehoods in the judge's report included the claim that the case was never reported to local officials. In fact, a week after the arrest, Sumlut's father-in-law had written appeal letters to the Kachin State Chief Minister, the Bhamo District governor and the Burma Army Battalion 321 commander.

What really happened to Sumlut Roi Ja is still unknown.

Human Trafficking (this contribution is taken from the chapter by Dr Lydia Tanner in *This Immoral Trade: Slavery in the 21st Century*).

Trafficking human beings for sexual slavery is a global business which has escalated in Europe in recent years, first hitting the British headlines in 2006, with a report by the BBC that women from Eastern Europe were being auctioned at a London Airport. This has led to awareness of the reality and scale of modern trafficking, with estimates of up to 2 million people traded across international borders every year, half of whom are children, with 70% of these females.

The suffering of these victims is taking place on our own doorsteps, illustrated by this story:

My life was normal and I was in my own little world, as any five-year-old or even younger child would be, until the very day my childhood was taken away from me. Two men who I will say would have been in their middle thirties came to see the lady I was living with.

I was called and asked to go with them. I was reluctant to go, but had no choice [but] to obey and moreover assumed that he was my father as the lady told me he would take care of me ... From the very first reaction I got from the man I understood and learnt not to talk and move until I was told to.

I was taken to a country that I had never been to; I had no knowledge about the language and culture. I wasn't able to ask where I was, as I wasn't allowed to have any conversation. I felt unwanted and hated by this man ...

This man would lock me down in the bedroom all day until there was a need for me to use the bathroom or he wanted me to do something for him. I was never to leave the house, open the door, or speak to anyone apart from him. I was also told to stop speaking my native language (as that was the only language I could speak at the time) and learn how to speak English and the other language spoken in the country that I was in.

From the age of five years I was to clean, wash, scrub, and tidy the whole house and would be punished if I failed to do it spotlessly and within the time given to me ... My duties included washing his clothes, scrubbing the kitchen and bathroom floor every day, dusting even when the house wasn't dirty. This increased as I got older. I was not allowed to go to school.

At the age of six I was forced to watch disturbing violent sexual movies and asked to do the same on him and in refusal I would be beaten up until blood was rolling on my face and body. I was six years old when I was raped repeatedly by him and his friend that lived with us. This man raped me about six times, and his friend raped me many times during the day when the other man wasn't around. He had the keys to the room so he always used to come in and threaten and rape me.

I had no way to escape or voice it out to anyone. Although I often heard voices coming from the flat during the day and most evenings, I was locked in the room and didn't get the chance to see anyone and I was really scared of this man as he always used to tell me that he would kill me if I told anyone what was happening and I wouldn't be believed. I tried to escape many times but the furthest I could go was outside the door and then I was caught and taken back. I honestly believed that they were capable of doing anything to me.

When I turned nine years I was forced to sleep with different men from all backgrounds. I was never given the money for what I did; settlements were made between the clients I was given and the two men I lived with. I never liked what I did but I had no choice but to obey because in refusal to comply I would have been assaulted both physically and mentally.

From the age of nine years to 15 years, I was assaulted, called names, insulted, used, and thrown anyhow by these clients and never had the right to complain to anyone. I never left the house until I was asked and I would be taken and brought back home. I never had the chance to walk, go to parks, or do activities as many do. This went on until I was brought to this country [Britain] and still forced to be a prisoner and sleep with men.

5. Migrant Domestic Workers

A variation on the theme is the abuse of many vulnerable migrant domestic workers by their employers. In the United Kingdom, the organization Kalayaan (the word for 'freedom' in Tagalog, a language of the Philippines) is striving to raise awareness of their plight and is campaigning for political initiatives to protect them. Many suffer gross exploitation with little or no payment; restrictions on freedom to move outside the house; sexual abuse and brutal intimidation, including threats of harm to their families in their home countries.

In their endeavors to help these domestic workers, Kalayaan have encountered difficulties with authorities and with the British government. For example, between May 2008 and August 2010, 37 domestic workers sought help from the police, accompanied by a Kalayaan staff member, but the police only recorded 12 cases, dismissing the rest as 'no crime committed.'

Recently, a change in immigration rules prevents vulnerable workers trying to escape exploitation by new employment to change employers, leaving them trapped. Kalayaan fear that this will encourage more trafficking and abuse of these vulnerable people.

What to Do?

Andrew Wallis, CEO of Unseen and Chair of the Centre for Social Justice (CSJ) Report on modern slavery in the UK argues: 'Any society is judged on the basis of how it treats its weakest members, especially the most hidden and silent.'

We who live in the freedom of Western liberal democracies have an obligation to challenge all forms of the continuing evil of slavery, both in our own countries and worldwide. And, especially, those of us who are Christians must never forget the Biblical mandate to do all we can to promote justice and freedom for all – and to break the bonds of oppression.

If the bondage of slavery in all its forms is to broken in our day, we need to break many other bonds: of ignorance, silence, interest, ideology, complacency, and complicity.

Bonds of ignorance

Far too many people are unaware of the existence of contemporary slavery and that it is increasing. While films like Slave can help viewers to understand the horror of enslavement, there is a risk that slavery is still seen as a historic evil of past eras. Therefore, we must all play our part in informing people of the contemporary reality and challenging them to engage with this issue as a matter of urgency.

Bonds of silence

We must shatter the silence and require our government to make representations to governments who currently deny, practice or condone slavery, such as in Sudan and Burma.

Bonds of interest

It is also essential to expose and challenge commercial interests which support, directly or indirectly, forms of slavery such as exploitation of child labor.

I have expressed my concerns that the Modern Slavery Bill going through Parliament at the time of writing this chapter does not adequately address the problem of the international dimension of contemporary slavery. Although attempts to address the issue of 'Supply Chains' which would help to identify and control the various forms of slavery and exploitation in the long, complex processes of production of international goods are welcome, the Bill still does not, in my view, deal adequately with the continuation of other forms of slavery in many countries today.

Bonds of ideology

Some contemporary slavery is ostensibly legitimated by ideology. For example, the massive slave raids in the war which raged from 1989 until 2005 were supported by leaders of the regime in Khartoum.

Arab traders from Sudan described on many occasions how political leaders from Khartoum would visit the lands bordering South Sudan with a rallying call to local people. They urged them to fight against the people of South Sudan, claiming this was a military 'jihad' and that they therefore had an obligation to attack the Christians. They also stated that those fighting would not be paid any wages but could keep the 'bounty of war' as recompense, including the 'human bounty' of captured women and children as slaves whom they were to convert to Islam.

While this interpretation of Islam is clearly not advocated by the majority of Muslims, it is very disturbing to see more recent manifestations in the policies of Islamist militants in Iraq and Syria. It is important that the notion of 'political correctness' or a fear of the label of 'Islamophobia' do not inhibit honest discussion of certain interpretations of Islam which are used to justify the practice of slavery over the past 1400 years.

In fact there has been more Arab enslavement of Africans than the horrific, and justly condemned, enslavement of Africans by white people in the Atlantic slave trade. Such open discussion is especially needed now, when Islamist terrorists are using their interpretations of Islam to continue policies of abduction, enslavement and forced conversion.

Ultimately, these are matters to be addressed within Islam. Nevertheless we should be ready to stand with those who try to promote interpretations of Islamic law which are compatible with our own contemporary Christian commitments to promote freedom for all and to protect the vulnerable from all violations of human rights, including slavery.

Bonds of complacency

It is very easy for many people to be so preoccupied with their own daily lives and responsibilities that they feel slavery is a distant phenomenon with no relevance for them. Therefore, although they may condemn it, they feel there is no obligation to take any action as there are other people and organizations with responsibility to do something.

However, as Christians, surely we cannot live in complacency, knowing that William Wilberforce's mission is still so far from being accomplished. His Christian faith impelled him to work tirelessly to achieve what he could, in his day, to eradicate this barbaric practice. Perhaps we should mobilize everyone in our sphere of influence – especially our churches – to 'look out' and to engage energetically.

Perhaps we all need to remember John Donne's famous challenge: 'No man is an Island, entire of itself; every man is a piece of the continent, a part of the main . . . Any man's death diminishes me, because I am involved in mankind. And therefore never send to know for whom the bell tolls: it tolls for thee.' Similarly, freedom is indivisible: every person denied freedom diminishes our freedom and challenges us to use our freedom to try to achieve theirs.

Bonds of complicity

It is often large organizations – international companies and governments – which turn a blind eye to injustice or refrain from robust, punitive responses.

For example, recent welcome reforms in Burma have led the international community to celebrate improvements and to encourage investment in some areas. Meanwhile, however, citizens in other parts of the country continue to suffer unscrupulous exploitation of their resources as well as gross violations of human rights, including forced labor and sexual slavery.

The famous saying, 'The price of freedom is eternal vigilance' suggests that as Christians we should be constantly vigilant. We need to look out for situations of complicity and be prepared to challenge them by speaking out and/or by actions such as boycotting the purchase of goods from firms known to be involved with exploitative labor policies.

Bonds of the enslaved

Until the bonds of ignorance, silence, interest, ideology, complacency and complicity are broken, it will be hard to break the bonds of the enslaved.

However, we can learn much from William Wilberforce: using publicity, Parliament, national and international diplomacy. We can also apply the principle of 'linkage': pressure on nations which currently support or condone slavery, with positive incentives for reform or penalties for complicity.

Every citizen in a free nation has the opportunity to speak out about the horror of contemporary slavery and to challenge governments to take genuinely effective action to do more to eradicate it.

In the fields of national and international diplomacy, we can use international agreements and organizations undreamt of in Wilberforce's day, including the Slavery Convention of 1927 and the Universal Declaration of Human Rights – agreed to by all nations except Saudi Arabia.

But many of its provisions, including Article 4 on slavery, are disregarded by certain member countries. The time is overdue to call such nations to account and to apply appropriate pressure to require them to desist from any form of slavery.

Conclusion

I finish by returning to the main focus of this chapter: enabling today's slaves to speak for themselves, and for those whose voices we cannot hear, because they are still enslaved.

I saw that one of the athletes in the 2012 London Olympic Games was running as an 'independent' competitor, not representing any nation. He looked as though he could be from South Sudan, so I made enquiries and discovered that it was the case and that this man had himself suffered the horror of slavery.

I asked if he would write a foreword to the book I was updating: *This Immoral Trade: Slavery in the 21st Century*. He graciously agreed and I conclude this chapter with some extracts from his powerfully moving account of his experience of his own slavery:

In 2012, I competed in the Marathon in the London Olympics. The qualifying race for the Olympics was the first formal marathon I had ever run. But I had spent my life on the run. Leaving my parents at the age of seven was not a matter of choice; it was a matter of survival ... the Arabs were abducting young children for slavery.

In the summer of 1995, a captain of the soldiers took me to a city called Muglad in Western Sudan, to work for him and his wife ... I was given a small bed and a small blanket. Part of the room was open so that the rainwater leaked through and my bed got wet ...

I did not worry about the wet bed or about the mosquitoes sucking blood through my black skin, because I knew at that point that I was a slave. I had no choice but to do everything I could to please my master and his wife. I was worried that if I did not, I would be instantly killed or sold to another stranger.

So I had to accept slavery and to hope God would save me one day ... I have escaped slavery twice.

Slavery is still a huge problem and threatens many lives today. It was a fundamental weapon used during the civil war between North and South Sudan. Freedom from slavery is a fundamental human right. For this reason, I strongly believe that people should learn about slavery in Sudan and across the world. I hope the world leaders can take this into serious consideration.

Guor Marial, Olympic Athlete, 2012 Olympic Games

As a Christian, I finish with a request for prayer: for the many millions of people who are now suffering the multiple horrors of enslavement, including torture and abuse, fear, loneliness, helplessness, humiliation, loss of loved ones and dread of what tomorrow will bring.

I also pray for families whose loved ones have been abducted into slavery, desperately worried, not knowing what is happening to them and if they will ever meet again. I pray for the perpetrators, that they will turn from their ways, seek forgiveness and find peace.

I pray for those who have escaped from slavery as they face so many challenges – sometimes rejected by their families, inevitably scarred in many ways, sometimes overwhelmed with fear of the future and in need of help, including resources for education or making a living, which may not be available.

And I pray for every one of us who is privileged to live in freedom that we may never take that freedom for granted but, in gratitude, strive passionately to promote freedom for all who are denied their freedom, in whatever ways God calls us.

We need to remember that as Christians, we are called to pray and to love – and prayer without deeds is dead, and love without action is dead.

Sometimes, we may feel so overwhelmed by the enormity of the problem and the complexity of the issues, that we do not know where to begin – so perhaps we just turn away. If you feel this way, I can sympathize!

Our charity, HART (Humanitarian Aid Relief Trust) is very small and we often feel overwhelmed by the enormity of our responsibilities for our many partners on frontlines of faith and freedom in very challenging parts of the world. Then we remember our motto: 'I cannot do everything but I must not do nothing'.

If we all do something, we really can make a difference!

Baroness Caroline Cox has been actively involved with Christian Solidarity International in the redemption of many hundreds of slaves abducted by the Government of Sudan and, with Humanitarian Aid Relief Trust (HART), working with victims of oppression and persecution who often suffer diverse forms of enslavement and exploitation. Her passion for freedom for all people is reflected in her book 'This Immoral Trade: Slavery in the Twenty-First century' and in advocacy in many contexts, including the British parliament.

http://www.hart-uk.org/

Chapter 9
Cargo – the Fight for Freedom, Past and Present
Paul Field

Imagine

Imagine you are a slave.

It's 1787. You are owned and you work fourteen hours a day, non-stop until you die. You will not grow old. You are subject to cruel punishments if you don't work hard enough and not paid a penny for your work. Collectively you plant, tend and harvest most of the world's crops.

Your slavery brings great wealth to a few, so change is unthinkable. However, in the back of a printing shop in London, twelve ordinary men are thinking the unthinkable. Unknown to you, a great wheel has begun to turn.

In Britain there are no caravans of chained captives or whip-wielding overseers stalking rows of sugar cane. Yet these twelve men will have to make ordinary people understand what goes on to bring them the sugar they eat, the coffee they drink and the tobacco they smoke.

And their campaign will work: in 20 years the world will be changed. William Wilberforce will champion the cause in Parliament, and the bill making the trading of slaves illegal will be signed into law on the 25th March 1807.

The next step of outlawing the ownership of slaves will take another thirty years, however. Wilberforce won't live to see it. Neither will you.

Now you are you again.

The great wheel has been turning for more than 220 years. Yet there are still at least twenty-five million people trapped in some form of slavery. Officially this is not the case, but new words, sleight of presentation, government complicity and more than a few blind eyes cloak the slavery that still exists. Poverty, desperation and ignorance disguise what lies ahead for those who find themselves tricked, traded, trafficked, kidnapped or conscripted.

> Now there is a slavery for everyone. Sex tourism, prostitution and pornography. Bonded or forced labor, caste-based slavery and the worst forms of child labor require an endless supply of slaves. The unprofitable are quickly discarded and replaced. They are disposable people. (Kevin Bales, *Disposable People*)

You and the rest of us will make the world what it will be in a hundred years. We're the ordinary people who need to know what lies behind the sugar we eat, the coffee we drink, and the clothes we wear. We need to break down apathy and prejudice and uphold the right of every human being to be free.

Finishing a task can be just as hard, just as inspiring as starting it. Only when there are no slaves can the wheel finally slow down and stop.

"Nobody is free until everyone is free." – Vivek Pandit

How Cargo came about

My wife Ruth is often the source of my best ideas. Sometime in the summer of 2005 she mentioned that 2007 would be the bicentennial of the abolition of the slave trade in Britain, and that the story of the abolitionists led by William Wilberforce could form the basis for a musical. As a composer and songwriter, I'm always looking for ideas and inspiration, and I enjoy the challenge of writing to a theme.

Those who abolished slavery were motivated by their faith. For me, faith has always been about who we are, not just something we do. The abolitionists' struggle is full of rich material, from the personal stories of the leading characters to the historical and political context of their campaign. Their legacy has shaped the world we live in today.

I began by buying a biography of Wilberforce and emailing friends and colleagues to test the water, canvassing for advice. Dr Nigel Shaw swiftly replied, 'If you want to know about Wilberforce and slavery, come to Hull.' Hull was William Wilberforce's home, and what better place to do research than the Wilberforce Institute for the study of Slavery and Emancipation (WISE) at Hull University?

Nigel arranged for me to meet with senior Professor David Richardson at WISE and I travelled up in trepidation, unsure how an academic expert might help me. Something created for performance and recording needs to be entertaining, engaging and credible as a piece of art, as well as informative and accurate in its historical narrative.

Professor Richardson was extremely helpful and encouraging and had an encyclopedic knowledge of the subject. He directed me to the main figures of the abolitionist movement and key moments in their campaign. He also gave me a reading list (just like being a student again) of the best books on the slave trade.

But one of his comments transformed my approach to the project and, more significantly, challenged my own priorities. Towards the end of our meeting he casually said, 'Of course, you won't forget about the unfinished business of slavery.'

Up to that point I had just been planning to write songs based on a historical account. It hadn't entered my mind that slavery was still very much alive and indeed thriving in the twenty-first century. I left Hull reeling from what I had heard about the extent of the contemporary trade in human beings and the many different forms it took. It was not just confined to distant third world countries; it was truly global and even happening on our own doorstep.

By the time I reached home I was determined that though this musical would be rooted in what happened more than two hundred years ago, it would also draw attention to the twenty-seven million people today in some form of slavery. People today who are tricked, traded and trafficked.

Merchandise with breakable hearts

While I was in Hull, by a strange coincidence, my sister Marion White was in conversation with the Christian leader, broadcaster and social activist Steve Chalke. Through hearing about his work through the Oasis Trust and a relatively new organization called Stop the Traffik, she was challenged to get involved and do something about trafficking. Part of her plan was to take a small group of women, mostly family members, to India to see Oasis' work with young girls who had been rescued from the sex trade.

The women travelled there late in 2006 to meet people working with the rescued girls and some of the girls themselves. It was no holiday, but a harrowing, life-changing experience. They came back with moving audio, photographic and video stories and a great determination to change things and raise awareness of what was going on.

Particularly powerful were photographs of my fourteen-year-old great niece with a girl of the same age who had been rescued from a brothel, where she had been kept locked in a cupboard-like room and only brought out to 'work'. In the photographs they shared beautiful smiles, belying their different life experiences.

Marion organized a tour for early 2007 in support of Stop the Traffik combining their stories and videos with some of the songs, music and narration that I was writing. So, the second half of 2006 was given over to the writing and production of this new musical called 'Cargo.'

Ruth and I decided to keep control of all aspects of the production, including finance, so we set about putting the creative and practical elements together. I contacted many people for advice and support including Pete Stanley (then with Stop the Traffik), Jeff Howarth at Anti-Slavery International (who checked my historical facts) and Ian Hamilton at Compassion UK, which supports some of the poorest and most vulnerable children in the world through a sponsorship program.

Compassion gave us some practical financial support for the CD production, and at Cargo performances throughout 2007, around three hundred people signed up to sponsor a child (which over an average of a ten-year sponsorship commitment represents around £700,000). We also were supported by the UK Human Trafficking Centre (UKHTC), particularly Nick Kinsella and Neil Brown.

Nigel Shaw and his wife Linda were hugely supportive of the project from the beginning. They suggested launching it in Hull City Hall at the end of March 2007 to coincide as closely as possible with the actual date of the Abolition of Slavery Act in 1807, and took on a project management role for that event. Since then they have been involved in many ongoing aspects of Cargo, including concerts, schools workshops and educational resources.

Creatively I decided that Cargo would use songs, music, narration, dance and visuals and that the live performances should involve as many people from the local community as possible. Choirs, musicians, dance and drama groups would be given the opportunity to be part of the events.

Originally, we planned just a few major performances around the country in cities that were central to the slave trade, such as London, Liverpool and Bristol. But although city councils were keen on hosting events to mark the bi-centennial, they were less forthcoming with financial help. We simply did not have the money up-front to fund and promote large events.

In the end, rather than a few big shows we ended up performing about a hundred concerts around the UK throughout 2007, playing to audiences from over two thousand in the largest venues, down to under a hundred in local churches. With hindsight, that was much better than a few big gigs. We reached far more people (around 30,000 over the year) and had much more personal contact and direct conversations about the issues of trafficking.

One of the most moving aspects of the eighteenth-century abolitionist movement is that it began with a small group of twelve men going against the tide. They campaigned tirelessly, without the aid of modern communications, internet or social media, to see the end of what was not just an offense against their faith but a fundamental injustice and abuse of human rights. Cargo tries to show that however insignificant we feel our influence is as individuals, enough small ripples together can create a tidal wave of change as they did more than two hundred years ago.

> *"Never doubt that a small group of thoughtful, committed citizens can change the world." – Margaret Mead*

It's a strange cargo that lives and breathes
that can feel the fear and pain;
A strange cargo that hears and sees
the depth of humanity's shame;
It's fragile like tears on the face of a child,
it's as soft as a lover's first kiss
and when merchandise starts with a breakable heart,
what strange cargo is this?

© Paul Field - from the song 'Strange Cargo' - Cargo

Looking back now, I'm amazed at the talent, commitment and positive attitudes of the group of artists who came together for the recording and performances. A huge thank you is owed to Coco M'bassi, Mike Haughton, Sadie Chamberlain, Dan Wheeler, Ruth Hughes and Springs Dance company (when we had enough space for dance!), to Richard Hughes for his work on the visuals, and especially to Sir Tom Courtenay who read the narrations for the recording. The venues were hugely diverse and sometimes downright difficult, but even when circumstances were not ideal, it was a privilege to work with them all.

I have many memories of Cargo gigs: the launch in Hull City Hall (almost completely sold out for two performances) where for the first time we saw the whole thing come together and the impact on its audience; Holy Trinity church Clapham – the home church of William Wilberforce and the place where the 'Clapham Sect' met and prayed together for the end of slavery; the Maritime museum in Liverpool; Brunel's 'Train Shed' in Bristol adjacent to the slavery museum; Blackpool Opera House, to an audience of three thousand with a choir of two hundred; a small church in Wisbech – Thomas Clarkson's birthplace; the UKHTC Conference in Leeds Armory Hall to several hundred police men and women and politicians from the UK and Europe.

All the performances, however large or small, were moving because of the response of the audience, many of whom (like me up until 2006) were unaware of the extent of modern slavery. We also met many inspiring people and heard heart-breaking stories along the way.

Neil Brown from UKHTC told the story of a fifteen-year-old girl from Lithuania which brought the issues of trafficking home to me in a very real way. Her parents had given her permission to come to London for 'the opportunity of a lifetime' believing she would be selling ice creams and learning English whilst being looked after and chaperoned by the very respectable couple who organized the trip. Within minutes of landing at Gatwick Airport (less than fifteen miles from where I lived at the time) she was sold for £400 in the arrivals hall. She spent the next three months being used as a sex slave and sold on in different cities around the UK (the price growing cheaper each time as the 'goods' became more shop-soiled) until she finally escaped through a toilet window in Sheffield.

> We can't turn a blind eye anymore and pretend that we
>   don't see.
> We can't nail our conscience to the floor and just try to
>   let things be.
> We can't pass the blame, we can't let it go,
> till everyone sees freedom's flag unfurled.
> We can shape the future.
> We can't let indifference rule the world.
>
> © Paul Field - from the song 'Blind eye' – Cargo

So many ripples have gone out from Cargo, and they continue to do so.

At the first Stop the Traffik gig (of which Cargo was a part) in Manchester Town Hall we met a young man called Ben Cooley who was so challenged by the presentation that he went on to set up Hope for Justice, now an influential charity working to uncover and abolish the hidden crime of modern-day slavery. My sister, Marion White, is on their board (www.hopeforjustice.org).

Trish Davidson came to Cargo in Bristol in 2007 and the following year set up Unchosen (a name taken from the song 'Midnight rain' from Cargo), an organization that mainly uses film to raise awareness of modern-day slavery. Their patrons are Ken Loach and Nick Broomfield (www.unchosen.org.uk).

In 2011 we took Cargo to South Carolina in the USA and performed several concerts with local singers, musicians and orchestra, jointly sponsored by a local church and Clemson University.

Many of the songs have been used by groups around the UK who work with trafficked people. At the time of writing, I am planning with WISE in Hull and author Kevin Bales, along with Nigel Shaw, to produce a new creative educational resource using music, dance, drama, images and video, for use in schools.

Today the whole world agrees that slavery is wrong. Yet it still exists and indeed thrives. The definitions may be more blurred, the issues more complex and the methods more subtle, but there are still fortunes being made through the exploitation of vulnerable people. Poverty, prejudice and unfair trade are at the root of this vulnerability and as such are inextricably linked with today's slavery.

The feeling that there is nothing we can do to change things is our most common excuse for doing nothing. And yet in the same way that twelve ordinary men started the great wheel moving, it is up to us to keep it turning, inch by inch, towards its final destination. We can never let indifference rule the world.

We can speak out, sign petitions, support organizations that work to end poverty, stand against prejudice and injustice, and act with our credit cards. We need to understand that our desire for ever-cheaper food and clothing may mean that someone, somewhere is paying the price with their liberty. Each penny we give and every fairly traded product we buy is one tiny victory in the battle against poverty and one small turn of the wheel on the road to freedom.

The only fair trade in people is no trade. We can make a difference.

Narration from Cargo © Paul Field (www.paulfield.com); on the Cargo project: www.paulfield.com/cargo; 'Maria/Midnight rain' and 'Blind eye' songs and videos from Cargo: www.paulfield.com/songsvideos.

Paul Field is a professional composer and songwriter with a particular interest in using his music to highlight social justice issues. He began work on 'Cargo' in 2006 intending it to be a musical built around the history of the abolitionists. As he got deeper into the subject, he became aware of, and shocked at, the extent of the modern slave trade, so his focus shifted to both celebrate the work of the abolitionists 200 years ago and also highlight the issue of contemporary slavery. He continues to include songs to raise awareness of trafficking in his solo concerts and is currently working on a major commission for the Wilberforce Institute at Hull University to produce a creative online resource for schools called 'Stolen lives', due for completion in September 2015.

http://www.paulfield.com/cargo.htm

Chapter 10
Twenty-seven Million
Beth Redman

Three years ago, my friend Christine Caine and I were both speaking at a women's conference in Belfast, Northern Ireland. My husband Matt and I have so much respect for the work that Chris and her husband Nick do around the world with the church movement Hillsong.

As we sat down to catch up with each other that June evening, little did I know Chris was about to deliver a wake-up call that would change the course of my life.

I was in the middle of the fog that comes with expecting one's fifth child. My passion was my family and writing books and speaking to a generation of teenage girls and young women. I talked about babies, America, travel, blah, blah, blah!

Then Chris told me for the first time about the work of A21 and the issue of human trafficking on the earth today. I was shocked. How had I not known about this? Where had I been?

I was so concerned with calling people to run after God and fulfill the purpose God has for them on the earth. Yet I neither knew nor acted on behalf of the poor, marginalized, 27 million slaves I shared the planet with.

As Chris spoke, I doubled over and wept to the point that I was almost sick. It was partly a sense of conviction about being asleep, but also a sense of being mobilized into action. My spirit was groaning; something had to be done. My life mission had changed forever.

Shortly after that conversation, my husband and I relocated from the US to the UK. Once the children were settled, I travelled to Greece to visit the A21 shelter. There I met young girls whose freedom had been stolen as they were trafficked from all over the world.

These precious girls were now safe and beginning the restoration process, thanks to the efforts of A21 and its supporters. Though still traumatized and in shock, they bravely told of the horror of their abduction and entrapment into the world of human slavery.

The night drew in, and we saw dozens of teenage girls working as prostitutes. As our car turned the corner towards our hotel, one young girl came out of the shadows in suggestive black clothing. Hands on her hips, she offered her body to each passing car. Her face was shattered and stony: a child no more, she stood on a filthy street corner after midnight. She should have been tucked up in bed, secure, treasured, safe, and innocent. Instead here she was, a victim of this modern evil, with one fearful eye on the pimp who stood not far away. A car pulled up beside her.

I could not get her face out of my mind as I went to bed. I was resting but her forced slavery continued. I realized that in order to save her we must tell everyone we meet that she exists, that human trafficking and slavery on the earth is worse than it's ever been before.

We must join forces with individuals, charities, corporates, government and statutory authorities and together rescue girls like her, one by one. We must find and prosecute her traffickers so that this crime will be exposed and punished, and slaves set free.

On a recent Sky2 documentary about human trafficking in Eastern Europe, Ross Kemp was interviewing a convicted sex trafficker. When asked how he felt about the women involved, the trafficker replied with a smirk:

> The girls are nothing. They are like footballs. You can just kick them and they'll do what you say. They are worth nothing. If one is destroyed, you can always get another. People are so much easier (to traffic) than drugs. The sentencing is a lot less.

We cannot be silent! Through my work with A21 I ended up in London for the launch of the *Slavery in the UK Policy Review*. It was sponsored by the Centre for Social Justice, an independent British think tank set up by Iain Duncan Smith to educate the public and promote the role of the voluntary sector. It involves figures from across the political spectrum and conducts research to provide evidence and seeks solutions for the causes of poverty.

Andrew Wallis, Founding Director of Unseen (UK) and CSJ Slavery Working Group Chairman spoke passionately. He said:

> In 2007 the UK celebrated the 200th anniversary of the abolition of the trans-Atlantic slave trade and in doing so led the world to recognize that slavery was trafficking in human blood and tears, in misery and suffering and that it had to stop for the sake of justice and humanity.
>
> Yet, here we are, with slavery rife amongst us. Whether we like it or not as a society, as individuals, we are in contact with slavery more often than we realize. They say we are all joined by six degrees of separation from any other human being on the planet. In all of these scenarios we are in much closer contact with slaves either here in the UK or overseas. None of us have clean hands.

We often hear much about human rights. But for there to be rights we have to acknowledge there are wrongs. I accepted the offer of chairing this policy review because I passionately believe slavery is wrong. This policy review will bring together all those who are involved in combating slavery so we can actually achieve what our forbearers hoped for – an eradication of slavery.

Two hundred years ago as a nation we led the world in saying: slavery is wrong, and we still aspire to that – to lead the world in combating slavery and bringing justice and freedom for those who are enslaved.

I realized through this launch that 'if there were no demand, there would be no slaves. The fact is that if you're a slave master today, you can always get another commodity. Tragically, the price of human slaves is the lowest it's ever been.'

As a response, we recorded a song called 27 Million, which was released as a single. It made it into the iTunes top 10 and even got to Number 1 in Bulgaria where A21 has a shelter.

We also wrote a pilot schools program for A21 which we launched in East London; it has been trialed across many parts of the UK. We hope to continue to raise awareness for this issue but also to raise funds to find and prosecute the slave masters and to rescue and restore the victims.

The good news is if you didn't know about this issue before, thanks to the united voices, hearts, talents, prayers and indignation of so many up-and-coming Wilberforces, you do now. It's time to set the slaves free!

Rather than being overwhelmed by the statistics, we should be outraged enough to do what we can. As Christine Caine said in her CNN blog:

My job is to help put tools in people's hands and say, 'Together we can stop that from happening.' Often, because we think, 'I can't do it all,' we end up being paralyzed. So we do nothing. But if we understand we all must do something, and we find the one thing that we can do, then together we will all make such a huge difference and we'll be able to put a stop to this.

Together – we can be the change!

Beth Redman is an evangelist, Dove Award winning songwriter, author and activist. She is based in Brighton with her husband, Matt, and their five children.

http://www.a21.org/

Chapter 11
Do You Want to Travel Fast?
Or Do You Want to Travel Far?
Antonie Fountain

Seven years ago, my wife came home with a bar of chocolate from a small Dutch chocolate company called Tony Chocolonely. Unlike most chocolate bars it had a very cool and unusual wrapper that looked like the old-fashioned comic books I've always loved. I looked more closely at the wrapper. In small print, in a yellow circle, were the words: 100% Slave-Free Chocolate.

I had no idea what this was supposed to mean. We'd abolished slavery ages ago, right? It wasn't as if there were little black children, forced to work as slaves to make our bars of chocolate, was it? What were they on about? This wasn't the 18th century anymore.

But it turned out, these 18th century practices were exactly what was happening. My wife – who worked for a development organization – explained the situation of child trafficking to the West African cocoa fields.

Tens of thousands of children, some as young as ten or eleven years old, were forced to work on cocoa plantations. For years. Without pay. In dangerous circumstances, wielding machetes, using pesticides without protective clothing. Needless to say, they weren't able to go to school.

As my wife was unfolding her story, I was stunned. In fact, I was so struck by this horrible fact that I sat in silence on my couch for more than an hour. Though I'd heard of a lot of injustice over the years, I knew I had to get involved in this myself. I had no idea how, but this was something that hit home.

I had been working at a marketing agency for almost ten years. I was doing well for myself. I was good at my work and had a career ahead of me, but my heart wasn't in it. A single bar of chocolate came in, and tore down the comfortable walls of my daily life. It screamed at me: there is more to life than this. You can make a difference.

Three weeks and a bizarre confluence of coincidences later, I was sitting in a bar in London. Opposite me was the director of Stop the Traffik, a new organization campaigning against trafficking in the cocoa industry. We were discussing the possibilities of me starting the Dutch chapter of the organization. organization

They had no money to pay my salary; I'd have to get that sorted myself. They had no on-the-ground presence in the country yet; it would be up to me to set that up too. The only thing they could give me was some rough information and possible actions for a grass roots movement, and a tie-in to a global and growing movement. And the knowledge that I would be actually trying to make the world a better place.

How could I refuse such an offer? I said yes, went back to the Netherlands, resigned from my job, and set forth on the craziest journey of my life.

Pretty soon, I started learning some important and painful lessons about myself. First of all, I wasn't very good at fundraising. Also, I wasn't very good at campaigning. But I believed in the change that needed to happen.

I also learned a few other important things. I had friends who believed in what I did, and instead of a salary, they started supporting me financially. I also learned that, although campaigning wasn't my thing, I was pretty good at talking to the big chocolate companies.

Companies like Mars and Nestlé started calling me up, wanting to meet with me. As our UK headquarters spearheaded campaigns, the companies wanted to connect with someone they could talk to in response. So, I started talking more and more with Big Chocolate.

At that time there was no progress at all. On the one side you had the chocolate industry, denying or downplaying the problem and claiming to be solving it all fine, thank you very much, no need to get involved. On the other side you had campaigning NGOs saying that nothing was being done at all. And the two did not meet.

I realized that it was quite useful to be a go-between in this stalemate. To translate what we as NGOs were asking to actual policy changes for the companies to get involved in. And others like me in other organizations were starting to have these conversations too.

Things are changing in the chocolate industry. Within just a few years, every single major chocolate company has acknowledged the problem of child trafficking in their supply chains. All have committed to plans to change their practices, although some plans are better than others.

Last year, I travelled to Istanbul to speak for the joint cocoa industry in Europe. They invited me, an activist, into their lion's den, and they listened . . .

A couple of months ago, I was in Brussels, in a session with some of the largest chocolate companies on the planet. They'd invited me to share my concerns, and to honestly think through how to solve them.

Just a few weeks ago, at the biggest sustainability conference on cocoa ever held, I was one of the main-stage speakers.

It took a lot of time. It took a lot of effort. But yes, things have changed.

Of course, they haven't changed enough. Trafficking still happens in the cocoa fields. Child labor and trafficking in their worst forms are still occurring daily in West Africa as their root causes are rampant. Almost every cocoa farmer in Côte d'Ivôire and Ghana – the world's main providers of cocoa – still lives in destitution and poverty. There is a very long way to go.

But we have come a long way, as well. And I've come to know a lot of the people working for the chocolate companies. The strange thing with getting to know people, is that you realise they are human beings too. You can have a beer with them. You can have a meaningful conversation about life, music, God, or parenting, just to name a few examples of our talks in the last months.

And I have come to realise that most of the people working for these companies are honestly trying to 'do the right thing.' The problem is that they are also trying to appease their stockholders and customers. And so they twiddle a knob here, tweak a setting there, and in little steps try to make things a little better.

But they're not able to see very far outside of the box. At least, that is my impression. You see, deep down I'm an absurd idealist. I honestly believe in Utopia.

I want to see a totally just world. One where everyone is treated properly, where everyone has a fair chance, where no one is left behind. I want to see human rights be considered a more important business principle than large stockholder profits. I want to see children going to school, before I see a company making a record profit.

I believe we should try to make a societal equivalent of Vincent van Gogh's Starry, Starry Night. We should be trying to build a world that is amazing and beautiful, for everyone, not just for the 'haves.'

In my conversations with chocolate companies over the years, however, I've realized that they are nowhere near that level of ambition yet. Most people, be they working for large companies, working for governments, or average consumers, are still at the level of 'Paint by Numbers.' So they are coloring in the spaces according to their numbers and it makes a picture, of sorts. The problem is that you can't just jump from 'Paint by Numbers' to being Vincent van Gogh.

I went to the Van Gogh museum last year with my daughter. She is six, and is one of his biggest fans ever. Last week she said she hoped Van Gogh could someday make as beautiful a painting of her as he had made of 'Camille.' She was very upset when we told her that Van Gogh died more than a century ago.

At the museum, we started looking at Van Gogh's earliest paintings. And they were horrible. The man obviously couldn't paint. In fact, he couldn't even draw. How did this man go from being a horrible draftsman to the stunning beauty that is 'Starry Night'?

The answer is very simple: he spent years practicing. And the same thing goes for us. We're going to need in-between steps if we want to get from where we are to where we want to be.

So the road from 'Paint by Numbers' to Vincent Van Gogh probably leads through a few lessons on the basics of painting. It's the same way for us. We first learn the basics. We go step by step. As the joke goes, 'How do you eat an elephant? Well, one bite at a time.' Change does take time.

The Indian philosopher Amartya Sen said, 'What inspires us is not necessarily the idea of a perfectly just world. Most of us don't expect that to be possible. What moves us, naturally enough, are the clearly solvable injustices around us.' So no one starts to paint thinking they're going to be Van Gogh. They just want to be able to paint a decent picture.

And this is what I have learnt when dealing with the chocolate companies.

Sure, I want a Van Gogh in the end. And I'm going to be fighting for that for a long time to come. But before the big players are willing to dream that big, you need to get them started on doing something about the clearly solvable injustices they are involved in at this very moment. Things they can quite easily remedy.

In the Netherlands where I live, 'Paint by Numbers' is called 'Everybody Can Paint.' And when we start looking at the clearly solvable injustices, everybody *can* paint. Just a few weeks ago, I was in conversation with someone from Mars, who said to me: 'There is no long-term business for unfair business. In the end, people will stop wanting to make your product for you.' They're starting to get it.

And the Mars and Nestlé's of this world might not be Van Gogh yet, but they're starting to get a pretty darn big step away from 'Paint by Numbers.' In fact, Mars was the first worldwide company to commit to 100% fair chocolate by the end of this decade. But it took many steps along the way. Many little bites of the elephant.

As I've said already, there still is a long way to go. We're really going to have to tackle the issues of poverty and inequality in the supply chain. And that will cost a lot.

It's going to cost the companies and their shareholders a share of their profit margins. It's also going to cost us, as consumers, as we start paying a realistic price for the products we buy. A price that actually allows farmers to send their children to school, instead of sending them to the fields.

The research and advocacy I'm involved in right now is showing that a cocoa farmer in West Africa might be earning just thirty per cent of what is needed to hit the absolute poverty line. In other words, if you'd increase their income by a factor of three, they'd still be absolutely poor. Is it any wonder they can't afford adult laborers? Unless we solve the problem of poverty in cocoa, we're not going to solve the problem of trafficking.

In fact, the average age of a cocoa farmer is just a couple of years short of his life expectancy. Younger generations are leaving the cocoa fields in droves, because the prospects are so bleak. Unless we manage to make cocoa an attractive prospect for new generations, the words of the man from Mars are going to be reality within just a few years. And that is going to have major effects on the amount of chocolate we'll be able to buy here in the West.

In short: unless we help the farmers make a decent living, chocolate is once again going to become a luxury product for the elite. If that won't make us get involved, I don't believe anything will.

The cocoa industry looks nothing like it did seven years ago. And I believe that it looks nothing like it will in seven years from now. The way that is going to happen is by continuously reminding them that they can be more than 'Paint by Numbers.' To not settle for business as usual. Because they can't afford to. And also because they can do better.

The only way to do that is by getting everybody together, and slowly pointing out which way to go. An old African saying says, 'If you want to travel fast, travel alone. If you want to travel far, travel with others.' That is also true if you want to change the system you're in.

Seven years ago in cocoa, people were not working together. People were trying to solve their own problems alone. Now, we're seeing massive collaborations amongst companies, between companies and development organizations, and between governments and companies. In fact, it's almost impossible to remember who's working with who any more.

It might be useful to streamline some of this collaboration. But people are starting to work together. And it's starting to make a change.

Nobody can do this alone. Whether you're fighting trafficking on West Africa's cocoa fields, or in the slums of Mumbai; you can't do it alone.

If you travel with others, it's a whole lot easier to eat an entire elephant. And who knows, you might actually end up painting a masterpiece along the way.

Antonie Fountain was Director of Stop The Traffik Netherlands for seven years. He now works as a freelance human rights activist, speaker and writer. As coordinator of the VOICE Network, he represents a major part of European civil society on sustainable cocoa.

http://www.voicenetwork.eu/

Chapter 12
A Community against Trafficking
Peter Cox

Being a Christian is all about going on a long, eventful journey. Many parts are exciting and enjoyable but unexpected pitfalls can emerge that can make the journey challenging and, for some, even terrifying. Perhaps this relates to my determination to do something about trafficking, or modern-day slavery as it is also known.

Christened as a child, confirmed as a teenager and educated at a church primary school, all the right kinds of seeds were sown for me. Yet in my busy twenties, when my work took me regularly around the world, I drifted away from being a proper practicing Christian. The quest to get financially established became the priority. Happily, when I got married in my thirties and my two children were born soon after, the desire to more openly exercise Christian values with my family was rekindled.

I have started this chapter with my own journey because there is no doubt victims of trafficking begin their journey hoping to improve their situation. With incredibly mixed feelings they set off from a place they know well, where they have friends and family, towards a promised land where they know no one but believe their lives will be changed for the better.

The expectations are high as they depart for the land of milk and honey. It doesn't take very long before they discover that these hopes will be cruelly crushed along their tortuous journey.

While serving on a church sub-committee set up to explore the needs of the vulnerable in our local community, I met Duncan Parker who was then working in International Development at the Salvation Army. Duncan spoke about the people he came across in his job and we were shocked. I remember thinking, 'In my thirty years in Croydon I haven't seen trafficked people, so where are they?'

I felt compelled to find out more and other Christians felt the same, so in 2005 the Croydon Community Against Trafficking (CCAT) was born. At our first meeting the five or six pioneers of CCAT met to plan a course of action, starting with what each person would like to bring to the party. I must have been slow on the uptake because as roles were suggested, hands went up much faster than mine to take things forward. Eventually there was only one role left. As I was the only person not to be allocated a position so far, I became Chair!

CCAT has moved on to become a respected charity in its own right with more than 1,300 members and 40 active volunteers. We are not overtly Christian, because to fight trafficking we want to engage with every member of our multi-cultural community. It became clear very quickly that this issue appeals to all members of our society whether they have any type of faith or not. Nevertheless, there is no doubt that we in CCAT operate with real Christian enthusiasm and values to bring more members of the public on board and to ensure the subject never slips from the authorities' agenda. Many well meaning organizations tend to bleat from the side lines but the CCAT approach is to campaign hard but also to work with the authorities to help them raise their game. By finding out where dubious places maybe operating and reporting them to the authorities we fill an important gap because victims are always hidden and the authorities have other priorities. CCAT also goes into schools to talk to our young people about modern day slavery. We must never forget that our young people are just as vulnerable in these difficult economic times. Much of our time is spent responding to requests from church and community groups who now have a better idea of what trafficking is all about but would not know it may be happening in their streets. We respond by spending time with them explaining how they might spot the signs of trafficking and to whom they should report their suspicions.

Sometimes it is hard for people in this country to understand how anyone can be duped into being trafficked. Maybe that is because, in spite of the hardships that some UK people suffer, their plight is not usually one of pure survival. Last year I had the opportunity to go to Moldova for a week to roll up my sleeves and do some hard labor to help develop a community project. Moldova is arguably the poorest country in Europe and is now independent from Romania and Russia.

I went to a rural village where about 1,300 people live in obvious poverty. Small cobbled-together houses with holes in the ground for outside loos, little employment opportunities, water obtained from local wells, most gardens just earth patches to grow food, no central heating, no national health service, no benefit system, just two teachers at one school, no phones (what's a mobile?), computers in just a handful of houses, no made-up roads, one bus a day to the nearest town/shop, no trains, etc. I hope you get the picture.

I was staying with some missionaries and was told of a widow in her late thirties with four boys, the oldest sixteen and the youngest six. When he was alive, her husband was the breadwinner, doing gardening and repair work around the village. How could she and her family survive without him?

Many young people travel to look for jobs when they reach about sixteen and this lady was approached by a gang master to offer her son work in the construction industry in Russia. She was promised regular money for the family from his wages which would enable her to feed her other younger boys. She agreed to this deal, but six months later she hasn't received any money and what is worse, she hasn't heard from her son. For all intents and purposes he has simply disappeared.

This Moldovan experience opened my eyes to how poverty and desperation force people to make dangerous decisions. There are evil ruthless people out there, ready to take advantage of the vulnerable so that they can line their own pockets. They have no conscience whatsoever. When I returned home, my determination to do something about trafficking via CCAT was increased. Do Christians get worked up over trafficking and slavery? I can assure you they do!

Trafficking tends to be considered an international crime as it often involves crossing borders. However, internal trafficking can occur within any country and is rife in countries like India. Consequently when CCAT talk to community groups, we always emphasize that UK people are also at risk. The homeless are often exploited, and care homes have been targets in recent years. Our unemployed young people are also very vulnerable in their quest to obtain a job.

Just imagine being turned down many times for positions and as a result, feeling depressed about work prospects. Then someone at a café or the library suggests there could be openings in the hotel, entertainment or fashion industries. At last someone is giving hope and apparently valuing a youngster who probably doesn't know where to turn to next.

This is why we feel our talks with schools are so important. Young people need to be aware that offers which sound too good to be true, probably are! Of course, opportunities that come out of the blue should be followed up, but not without caution and checking out carefully the conditions involved.

There is no doubt that being heavily involved with CCAT has a positive knock-on effect for my life overall. I meet with some very busy people who feel so passionately about stopping trafficking that they contribute much of their free time to CCAT – I have to warn them not to let it impinge on their family life!

Although we must do things to a professional standard to move the charity forward, we also need to be fair to our volunteers. I pray often for guidance on what I should reasonably expect from others. In a world where communication is often instant and continuous, action from CCAT is invariably required equally quickly. Yet timescales are invariably negotiable so I've learnt to be calm and measured in my responses.

I know a person quite well who has recovered from being trafficked and subjected to slavery. Jane (not her real name) is not British but has remained in the UK, where she is now becoming part of our community. She has a good job and goes to a local church, mixing in with other young people easily.

Seeing how a person's situation can change inspires me to do more to help others out there. There could be many others like Jane in our neighborhoods, hidden away in conditions of exploitation but we do not notice them. I just hope this book will help us all lift our heads above the parapet, and take more notice of what is going on so we can save others who may be suffering. I certainly plan to continue to do my bit no matter how small that may be.

It was 2004 independent research under the Poppy Project indicating his home borough of Croydon was particularly vulnerable to trafficking that made Peter Cox want to find out more and do something about this human tragedy. Inspired by others who felt equally strongly, he became Chair of Croydon Community Against Trafficking and the charity is now considered a best practice model of a community making a positive difference. In 2014 Peter was honored to be presented in the House of Commons the Marsh Christian Trust Award for "Outstanding Contribution to the Fight against Human Trafficking."

http://theccat.com/

Chapter 13
The Salvation Army's
Fight against Slavery
Anne Read

Since we started back in the 1870s and early 1880s, the Salvation Army has been involved in anti-trafficking. We've always been committed to this issue, but over the last few years we've been responding in new and creative ways that are appropriate to our resources and to the need. And internationally this is a high priority for us.

Here in the UK we've appointed an anti-trafficking response coordinator and I am the second person to hold that position. So I co-ordinate our response to this whole issue of human trafficking.

As a Salvation Army Officer I'm an ordained minister of religion, commissioned to go where ever they choose to send me and do whatever they ask me to do. I've been an officer for about thirty five years in inner-city situations, and in training work. I qualified as a teacher before I became an officer.

A few years ago I was responsible for a large Salvation Army church in Oxford Street. I was due for a change of appointment and wanted to write to the leadership, asking if there was any possibility of working in the area of anti-human trafficking. It felt as if it would be a really great privilege to do so, but I never wrote the letter.

One day in 2009 I was called to come and speak to them, and the extraordinary thing is that they asked me whether I would take on this responsibility. I couldn't believe my ears, because I hadn't told them, but they sensed it and God knows my heart.

That's actually been quite important because sometimes the role has been very demanding and difficult. I feel I'm in this not just because the Salvation Army think that I can do it, but that God sorted it for me. That has really encouraged me and helped to give me strength to carry on.

I had quite an unusual, unconventional upbringing because my parents were also Salvation Army officers and I was brought up in men's hostels. For ten years I lived in a boys' approved home where my parents were warden and matron. My parents weren't preachy at all; they lived the gospel in front of me. And those people most of all needed to hear good news because their situations were so difficult and dire.

So it feels as if my childhood and other officer roles have made me what I am and have prepared me for this appointment. It's been a continuum of preparation for this particular role at this particular time.

The survivor's journey

Every survivor of human trafficking has their own story and the things that they've experienced before being trafficked contribute to the way they cope, or struggle to cope. So every person's different. The common factors are often in the area of somebody's value as a human being and their autonomy.

It seems to me that human trafficking tries to rob the individual of their sense of value, even their own character. So very often the victims feel as if nobody cares about them and that they are of no worth. And probably the most important thing at the start is to give survivors of trafficking back that sense of self-worth to empower them again to make decisions.

Some victims have been so entrapped in their situation, so under the control of their trafficker that they are almost incapable of making even the smallest decision for themselves. Helping somebody to begin to feel that they are of immense value is certainly part of the process of their recovery.

One of the very first things we do for a victim is to take them from their place of rescue or the place where they've escaped, to the place of safety, and we provide transport through a very large team of volunteers. In doing this we show the victim that somebody cares about them, so this physical journey to a safe house is also the start of the journey to their recovery.

They begin to realize that there are people who do care, who are bothered enough to make this journey with them. Often there's no common language to share long conversations, just that opportunity to show kindness and compassion.

I'd like to think it's just the beginning of a window opening for them, showing there is light ahead and they will come out of this dark experience. And often it's those little things that begin to communicate this message that they are of value and people do care.

We also provide welcome packs for survivors when they arrive at the safe house. It's just a very little aspect of the service we provide victims, but again we think that having a nicely wrapped gift available to them when they arrive communicates once again that people are concerned and are bothered. I think it is another small way of giving somebody back their sense of self-worth.

Another thing that is fundamental is this sense that we aren't just providing what the survivor needs, but helping them to access what they need to move on. We don't do everything for them, but we're there with them as they start to make decisions again for themselves, sometimes very everyday things but also long-term decisions like what they're going to with the rest of their lives.

Rebuilding trust

Anyone who works with a victim of human trafficking will soon discover that there's no reason at all why they should trust anybody. It's often the experience of trusting somebody that has led to the trafficking in the very first instance. The probability is that someone has promised them a dream, in the form of a job or a future or a relationship and that hope was betrayed. That initial breakdown of trust starts their trafficking experience and then it will continue from there.

That's one of the reasons why it's very hard for somebody to tell their story. They've probably been told that they can't trust the police, that nobody is to be trusted, and if they tell anybody, they'll be in serious trouble. So for all kinds of reasons they'll be very nervous about trusting anybody.

Our responsibility

We are becoming more aware that human trafficking is not just something's that is happening far away or in big cities or in other countries, but it's happening in our communities. And as we become more aware of that I think there's an enormous responsibility on us as individuals to respond.

So we need to be alert to anything that is suspicious, that indicates that somebody is being controlled or has been harmed in some way or is frightened. I think it's a very British thing to mind our own business but I would strongly encourage people not to mind your own business, make it your business. There's more harm to be done by not doing anything than there is by doing something.

I would encourage people to respond if they think someone is in any way in danger. Don't hesitate to call the police; they are very victim-focused nowadays so they understand this issue. You can also do a quick search and find anti-trafficking sites with indicators about what to look for and how to recognize if a person might be held in slavery. If there's something that makes you feel uncomfortable, do something, don't do nothing.

I think we all have a responsibility to address the ways in which we can be complicit in issues around exploitation and people being used as slaves. Whether in the things we buy or the services we access, are we contributing to this terrible injustice?

It's a challenge for all of us. If a service or an article is cheap, we need to consider why and what is behind this. Making a different choice could mean the difference to somebody, either close by in our community or on the other side of the world. Let's make our choices good choices.

If the heart of trafficking is that fact that somebody has been bought and sold, used and abused, left feeling worthless as a human being, our role is somehow try to help them to understand the immense value that they have as God's creation. They are a child of God, someone who is made in his likeness, who is crowned with glory and honor, who was created to be a little lower than the angels. And some of us have the opportunity to walk with the survivor on the road to that discovery.

The Salvation Army's involvement

The Salvation Army has been involved in anti-human trafficking since the early 1880s for sure, and we were involved in a very high-profile case that went to the Old Bailey. We worked with WT Stead, the editor of the *Pall Mall Gazette*, a very well-known London newspaper, and other social reformers to raise awareness that women and girls were being bought and sold into the sex trade at that time.

A girl called Eliza Armstrong was thirteen years old and the Salvation Army bought her for five pounds from her parents. Of course she then went to a safe house, but the Booths and WT Stead were charged with procurement and went to the Old Bailey. The

Booths got off on a technicality, but WT Stead was sent to prison for six months for that offence. However, the articles he wrote in the *Pall Mall Gazette* created a huge response around the country.

The Salvation Army went on to campaign to see the age of consent raised from thirteen to sixteen years of age, where it is now. They gathered nearly four hundred thousand signatures, and that was in the days when you couldn't just sign by clicking! So it was a huge achievement to launch and eventually win that campaign to try and ensure the safety of more girls in this country.

Since 2011 the Salvation Army has had the government contract to manage support for all adult victims of human trafficking in England and Wales who want and need this. We do that as the prime contractor, through working in partnership with thirteen other organizations to provide a service to around three hundred victims of trafficking at any one time.

Most of those are in safe houses, but some in outreach accommodation. The majority are women but there are also a large number of male victims of labor exploitation and also families. Some of the families that we support are very large family groups.

A survivor's story

Miriam saw her own father being murdered in Rwanda. She had no one else to trust, and so when her uncle offered her a job in England, she trusted him. But when she got here she was met at the airport by a man. After having had two days just being able to sleep and rest, he came into her room and said, 'I want you to give this man whatever he wants.' She asked, 'What do you mean? Cook for him?' – that was the level of her naivety.

Then it emerged that she had to sleep with him, and as time went on she was forced to have sex with five, six, seven, eight men day after day. She was scared for her life because when the trafficker said to her, 'If you don't do this, I will kill you,' she really believed him. She'd seen her parents being killed and they had tried to kill her too, so she had no doubt that this would happen to her if she didn't do what was asked of her.

So she had no choice until the day when the door was left open, and for the first time she had the opportunity to escape. She ran and ran and ran until a policeman found her sitting in a park and offered her help, which came in the form of accommodation at a Salvation Army safe house. Miriam has now left that safe house and is hoping to train as a social worker. She is beginning the job of rebuilding her life.

Supporting survivors

Here in the UK the government contract ensures that all victims of trafficking who are referred though their mechanism receive certain rights under the European convention. These include safe accommodation, counseling and emotional support, and advice. This might encompass legal advice and immigration advice which would include support in recovery of documentation and anything that will help the victim to move on following their experience.

The support is given for a period of forty-five days, although this can be extended. During that time the victim will be encouraged to consider their options when they leave the service. Many survivors wish to stay in this country and so we advise them as to how that would happen or how they might be supported in returning to their home country if it was safe to do so.

There's always more that can be done, but the system does ensure that the victims do get some support. As we work together with all of our partners who are committed to working with victims, value is added to the contract. It all goes a long way to helping the victim to rediscover their value and also start to make a contribution again to their communities and to wherever they choose to settle.

Major Anne Read is The Salvation Army's Anti-Trafficking Response coordinator and has held her position since 2009. Anne originally trained as a teacher, but for the past 34 years has worked as a Salvation Army officer (Minister and Leader) in a variety of different and challenging roles. Anne is a member of a number of UK based Anti Trafficking groups including the Home Office Joint Strategy Group and the UK Human Trafficking Centre Advisory Group. She also represents the United Kingdom and The Salvation Army on European and Global task forces bringing issues of human trafficking to the fore for a wider audience.

http://www.salvationarmy.org.uk/human-trafficking

Chapter 14
A Safe House for Survivors
Tina English

'It's the police,' I whispered to my colleague. What happened next on a so-far uneventful night would change the direction of our lives. It would also be life changing for many women who had survived the horrors of human trafficking.

I was working as a volunteer for a charity initiated by my church, a residential program for young women with life-controlling issues such as alcohol and drug dependency, self-harm, depression and unplanned pregnancies. The women lived at the house and got support to help them rehabilitate and recover, supported around the clock by trained staff and a team of volunteers. I loved seeing the transformation in the women's lives – it was a privilege to be part of it.

We already had links with the local police as some women we supported were ex-offenders and been involved in criminal activity, but it was unusual to receive a call so late at night. The officer explained that they had a Chinese girl who was a victim of trafficking. My immediate reaction was that she should be taken to Accident and Emergency, thinking she had been involved in a road traffic accident!

The police knew we had a safe environment to care for young women, and with nowhere else to keep her apart from a cell at the local police station, they appealed for our help. We were shocked to hear of this girl's heart-breaking plight and offered her accommodation.

A traumatized and frightened young woman was delivered to the house later. She didn't speak English and was extremely nervous. Her age had been assessed at between 18 and 20 years. She had no identification and was brought into our care with only the clothes she wore. My heart went out to this beautiful girl who had experienced a nightmare at the hands of the traffickers. She was exhausted but grateful for a safe place to stay.

Once she was settled for the night I returned home and searched the internet for all the information I could discover about human trafficking in the UK. I couldn't believe the scale of the problem. I had known of Stop the Traffik, a charity which had a mission to raise awareness, but failed to understand that it was happening on our own doorstep. My eyes were opened, and so grew the seeds of my passion to do what I could to help the victims of this abhorrent crime.

My journey

During this period I was working full time as a manager of a national High Street bank. This was my lifelong career, having been employed by the same bank for over 30 years. I was one of the first women in my area to study banking exams. Banking was definitely a 'man's world' during the 1970s and women's careers traditionally ended with marriage and children, except for those who were retained in secretarial and administrative roles.

I combined my career with bringing up my three children, and once they were more independent, I began studying at a local university. Doing 'women's studies' further fired my passion to see women play their part in society and reach their full potential, with education and opportunities enabling them to live worthwhile and fulfilled lives.

I was fortunate that my church had initiated the residential project to help young women who needed support to get their lives back from desperate situations. I had the opportunity to get involved from the start as a volunteer and gave my time after work in the evenings to help the women.

The young Chinese girl settled in, was provided with new clothing, underwear and toiletries and surrounded by love and care to help her recover. She was so grateful for the support she received, and we were glad to be able to protect her at this desperate point in her life.

After a few days, following a meeting with the police investigators, it was decided to move her to a safer location in another part of the UK. It wasn't wise to keep her in the same city where she had been rescued, as the perpetrators were still around and keen to find where she was. It also put both staff and other residents at risk, so she was moved in a covert operation to a safe house. The traffickers would go to terrifying lengths in order to find her, because she was a very valuable commodity to them.

In 2006 United Kingdom Human Trafficking Foundation (UKHTC) for EU nationals was formed to help fight the growing crime of trafficking. We were offered the chance to visit and subsequently speak to the team there about the work they did and the provisions in place for survivors. Nick Kinsella and his team were victim focused and had set up a victim fund to help support the growing number being rescued.

Our reputation for victim care grew as we had a dedicated team with a number of volunteers passionate about loving victims back to life. We started to develop even stronger links with UKHTC and the dedicated team at the center, sharing their commitment to fight the phenomenon of human trafficking. Despite minimal funding we were prepared to step in at a time of need.

At this time the main victim care provider in England and Wales was the Poppy Project based in London. They had a government contract to provide accommodation and support for a 45-day reflection and recovery period. The victims that were identified were referred to Poppy and housed in accommodation in the South East of the UK.

The following months I spent time finding more information about the scale and effects of human trafficking in the UK and also internationally. I was astounded. I set about raising awareness and learning about victim care provision. I was particularly concerned about the lack of criminal convictions and how the perpetrators were able to get away with such inhuman treatment.

My sense of injustice gave me the energy to fight on behalf of survivors, devoting my time to see care of victims improved. Many victims, vulnerable men, women and children, were criminalized and sent to prison or detention centers after experiencing exploitation, violence and abuse. The more I discovered and saw, the more I was spurred on to take action and get involved.

Care for victims

We continued to care for victims; more women were referred as well as a family from an Eastern European country. We helped them to feel safe and secure and access medical services, and supported them through the asylum process and police investigations.

I was so affected by the women's stories. Each one was different, but the horror of their experiences really strengthened my desire to make a difference. I was so saddened to hear what they had been through.

Initially there were tears of relief in a place of safety, and then we needed to deal with their shame and night terrors that followed. To be there at these times for the women is precious, and forms bonds that cannot be broken. It is such a privilege to witness the transformation when trust is gained and hope is restored.

As we gained a reputation for caring for victims of trafficking, three Romanian girls were referred to us who had been in prison in the UK for nine months for the part they were alleged to have played in a trafficking case. During this time it became apparent that they were actually vulnerable girls who had been exploited and trafficked by a criminal gang. When the girls' true stories were revealed, they agreed to be vital witnesses to help police prosecute the actual perpetrators.

The young women were not only traumatized by their experience with the traffickers, but also by their time in prison. They needed help to settle in their environment and to know they were safe in a loving, caring family environment. The police were able to contact their families via the Romanian police to let them know they were safe and well. One family had already held a memorial service believing their daughter to be dead; she had been missing for over two years.

The women arrived in a desperate state, but it was a joy to see their journey progress and to discover their true fun-loving personalities. Previously held together by the same gang of traffickers, now they were able to enjoy their friendship in freedom, doing things that other girls their age did. They enjoyed shopping, watching movies, going into town and exploring their new hometown, and making new friends.

Support in court

Many hours were spent supporting them through medical appointments and frequent police interviews. The whole process of the court case took many months. The police required the women to be kept in a safe environment and supported throughout, because they were vital witnesses in a serious case. This proved to be a traumatic time for them all.

I was working closely with the investigating officers in Manchester and can only commend their approach and care for the women.

Although it was first thought impossible, we successfully fought for them to get their criminal convictions quashed, which was a great relief for us all. During this time I furthered my calling to working with survivors of human trafficking, and dedicated as much time as I could to help. I decided to reduce my hours at work, which enabled me to be more involved.

The Romanian girls had all been given twelve months' leave to remain in the UK, enabling them to obtain National Insurance numbers and the right to gain employment. My position at the bank as a Business Relationship Manager meant I had many contacts in the business community, so I was able to help two of the women gain positions as cleaners in local offices. The other one decided to work part time at the café in the church-run community center.

The opportunity to work and earn their own money helped the women become more independent. With assistance they were able to move into their own rented property, which they shared. Seeing them gain confidence, become self-reliant and an active part of the community was a real pleasure. To come from a place of despair to where they were now was an amazing transformation.

When the court case in Manchester eventually started, I was able to travel with each of them on separate occasions over a period of a number of weeks. They had already made lengthy statements which were videoed and shown to the court. They were then able to answer any questions during the trial in a separate room via live video link. Reliving their violent and abusive experiences really affected them, and they needed a lot of reassurance and support to know they were safe. The girls were surrounded by a compassionate team who helped to see them through this stressful time.

I was able to sit in the public galley throughout the trial, hearing the horrific treatment all the women had been subject. To understand that they had survived so much cruel abuse was heart-breaking, and to be part of their journey to recovery was humbling.

The main trafficking gang were found guilty on numerous counts and duly sentenced to serve time in prison. The longest sentence was 21 years which was a great result for us all, particularly the survivors and the police. Following the case the women settled and started living their lives in the knowledge that they were truly safe. The criminals were going to be out of the way a long time.

The detectives involved were very grateful for all our help supporting the women and ensuring they travelled to court to testify. Later, I was awarded the Divisional Commander's Award by Greater Manchester Police in recognition of outstanding work throughout the case. It was a great honor to be recognized for the part I played in seeing justice done.

Developing the safe house

During the time that followed we were taking care of an increasing number of referrals. We supported mainly women from EU countries, including Lithuania, Slovakia, Romania, and Hungary. All had been confirmed as victims of trafficking and were helping police bring the traffickers to justice.

At this time, we decided to open a further house for women and keep the original house solely for the purpose of victim care. It had now become a safe house and extra vigilance and security was put in place.

Helping women during the traumatic time of a major court case is vital. Being a witness and facing events that have affected them deeply can be distressing, but with love, and care they can overcome fear and rise to the occasion. Some victims choose not to assist the police, which obviously hinders efforts to prosecute offenders, but the women are free to make their own decisions at all times.

We became aware that during the next twelve months the government contract for victim care was up for tender and wanted to be part of this provision. We had the experience, policies and procedures in place to provide a specialized level of care.

A colleague and I were invited to victim care meetings at the Home Office in London and made many trips to the capital, familiarizing ourselves with other care providers including Poppy and TARA. We were becoming knowledgeable about processes, statistics and government policy. Gaining all this information about first responders and the National Referral Mechanism increased our confidence in being able to provide excellent ongoing specialized care to victims.

The number of victims being recognized was increasing and many were high-need cases requiring support. During one visit to London we were invited to the Serious Organized Crime Agency (SOCA) as plans were being made to move UKHTC to their department in Birmingham.

Raising awareness

I worked closely with a police detective who specialized in cases of trafficking. We had many speaking engagements arranged to address women's groups and churches and the Conference of the Soroptimists. I welcomed any opportunity to raise awareness about the scale of human trafficking both here in the UK and internationally, and speak of the real horror of this crime.

We also recounted the many hilarious moments we had working with women from all different cultures, ages and backgrounds, particularly as went on trips to local places of interest.

Once while visiting a wildlife park, we were feeding bread to the ducks when a large stone whistled past my head aimed at a rather plump goose. The stunned bird quickly recovered, but the look of horror on the other visitors and children there was obvious. One of our innocent young women thought it would have been a welcome addition to the pot for dinner. In her remote African village, if you didn't catch the food, then you didn't eat.

There were many fun times of shopping, sightseeing, and generally starting to live a life of freedom and security. Seeing how the women lived and socialized together was always interesting. Cooking and trying different food from all over the world was a special time of sharing and forming lifelong friendships. Relaxing in the lounge seeing women from Africa, Asia and Europe dancing, singing and laughing together is a joy to behold. Special times like this never leave you and are so enriching. I believe I had the best job in the world.

Visit to Romania

My interest in Eastern Europe, and the lives of the women at risk of being trafficked grew. This developed into the decision to lead a group of women to visit Romania and find out more of the situation at first hand. We were hosted by the Nightingales Project, a British charity working in an area where poverty was rife and many young girls were at risk. They were launching a project aimed at educating young people in local schools about the risks of trafficking. There was also a mentoring scheme where the young people from a local high school helped disadvantaged youngsters.

During this week we were able to work within the schools. It was a poor area but we were made welcome and so much interest was shown in everything we had to say about the horrors of human trafficking.

There was a distinct lack of adults in the community as the majority were working abroad, mainly in Italy and Spain, able to earn considerable more money than at home. Many children were left in the care of siblings or grandparents, leaving them vulnerable and at risk.

Nightingales do amazing work setting up after-school clubs and activities to help young people in the community. They also have safe house provision for survivors returning to their home country. Their work continues and goes from strength to strength, making a difference in the lives of many people.

As part of the program during my time in Romania I was able to visit a high security prison for women. It was very rare opportunity as I was the first woman from the UK given access to speak to all the female prisoners. I explained how seriously the crime of human trafficking is taken by the British government and the police.

Then I told them the true story of one particular Romanian victim and the suffering she endured at the hands of the traffickers. Following my talk there were many women in tears and begging forgiveness. I was later told they were in prison following convictions for recruiting young girls to be sexually exploited overseas.

Developing the work

In June 2011 the Government contract for the provision of victim care in England and Wales was awarded to the Salvation Army. Our safe house was sub-contracted to provide accommodation and specialist support 24 hours 7 days a week. At this stage I was able to leave my work at the bank and devote all my time to caring for survivors. It was a dream come true. We had all worked hard to get to this point and I was committed to meet and support these women.

From the start of the contract we accepted referrals and new women arrived on a daily basis. They originated from many different countries. I was able to talk to the African women about my visit to Ghana and it helped them feel at ease knowing I had experienced first-hand life in an African community. Making the women feel at home, safe and secure and develop trust is so important. It is vital to respect their cultures, respect them and understand they need time, patience and loving care to recover.

The government provision in England and Wales is for a 45-day reflection and recovery period. Potential victims are identified by first responders, often the police or health care professionals, then referred to the NRM (National Referral Mechanism) and notified to the Salvation Army. The UKHTC (for UE National) or the Home Office (Non-EU Nationals) will look at each case and make a decision. If there are reasonable grounds to believe that the individual is a victim, then they are entitled to the 45-day care provision. During this period the Home Office or UKHTC will investigate the case and make a conclusive decision.

Each case is individual and treated as such in provision of care. Every woman is allocated a dedicated case worker and a risk assessment carried out. When a woman is referred there is generally only a basic overview of their situation and background provided by the first responder.

Most women arrive at the safe house late at night, often having been moved from a police station or detention center. Most arrive traumatized, tired, and afraid with just the clothes they are wearing. Often they believe they are being moved to a prison. The first few hours are spent reassuring and welcoming the women into their new home.

The other women are encouraged to be friendly and prepare food for them to share. When the woman is shown her own bedroom with fresh bedding, new underwear, clothes and toiletries there is a great sense of relief as they begin to realize that they have reached a place of safety.

After a good night's rest, an assessment is conducted to decide if medical intervention is needed. Every woman is offered full screening at the local medical center and at the G.U. clinic. It is vital that health care is addressed and the right medication prescribed as necessary. Dental work is often required as this may have been an area neglected for many years.

Once health issues are addressed, we find out the future plans, hopes and desires of the individual woman. These often include help appointing a legal representative and support through the asylum process (for non-EU nationals), and accompanying to visits to solicitors and the Home Office. Assistance is often given to help trace family or help with the process of returning home. Contact with anyone is restricted as it is important that the whereabouts of the women or the location of the safe house is not compromised.

In the 45-day period there are many areas to address including psychological issues. At every stage the woman is supported, reassured and cared for. Most women will take advantage of the specialized counseling sessions that are available to help them women deal with the trauma of their past experiences. They have proved invaluable.

Often there is police involvement where the woman has been rescued from a situation or they have reported the crime to the police. It is again important to support women through this time, because giving statements and talking to the police is always a cause of anxiety and fear.

In a relatively short space of a few weeks many practical things have to be done to help each survivor. What I have loved about the job is that all this can be done in a warm, caring environment. This helps the recovery time both in the safe house and beyond. Trust is built, and friendships develop.

Many women from EU countries such as Romania, Slovakia, Hungary and Czech Republic now choose to return home. The majority have no form of identification, passports having been retained by the traffickers. An appointment at the relevant consulate office in London is arranged to obtain travel documents. This follows a full assessment to ensure they have a safe place to return to, either their home with family (often they have children) or maybe a specialized safe house in their country of origin.

During time at the safe house there is plenty of time to relax and rest. The house is a homely environment, good food is provided and everyone cooks and shares traditional dishes. Much laughter and fun is common. There is peace and quiet in their own bedroom if needed, or time to be sociable and get to know others. Communal eating areas and a shared TV lounge ensure no one ever feels alone.

Volunteers provide friendship and outings, jewelry workshops with local students, English and IT classes. The women are encouraged to help each other and friendships made during this time continue and flourish when they are living in the community. Donations from many supporting organizations provide continuing supplies of clothes and toiletries.

With a growing number of women settling into the community, we were continually grateful to the dedicated volunteers supporting the women. A significant number of women referred to the safe house were pregnant. We ensured they linked with all the relevant agencies to get the maternity care they needed.

One particular volunteer devoted all her time to helping the pregnant women before giving birth and also being a birth partner. She provided them with a cot, blankets, clothes etc. This amazing lady had built up so many contacts of people willing to donate baby items. She has been able to provide all the equipment a new mum needs – she's an angel on earth.

The women are so grateful for the continued love and care she gives them. Having a new baby, especially when no family is around, can be a very scary, lonely time for a single mum. This wonderful lady is dedicated to the women, their babies and their continued care.

With so many moves, ongoing help is needed with housing arrangements, benefits, bank accounts and money management. Just understanding the systems and how agencies work in the UK can be confusing for anyone, let alone a lone woman from another country. A few of us continued to help women beyond the 45-day period and also try to link them to other charities and NGOs that could assist further.

We all worked long hours helping to arrange housing with the local authority, decorate and furnish flats, sort benefits, and help finding employment opportunities. The workload was increasing as we continued to support more and more women in the safe house.

A colleague, who was also a caseworker, began recruiting willing people from her church to volunteer and help out. A growing need was recognized. We could see the difference this support meant to the women. Moving on for them became a pleasure, knowing they were surrounded by people who cared, and furthermore were willing to devote time to ensuring they were being settled and still provided for in the community.

The Snowdrop Project

Over the coming months my colleague Lara Bundock worked tirelessly with a team of other dedicated people to see the launch of the Snowdrop Project, the first of its kind in the UK to provide ongoing support to survivors of human trafficking. The project's innovative work was recognized by the British government's Home Secretary and the Human Trafficking foundation and won the 2013 Marsh Award at the House of Parliament in London.

The Snowdrop Project relies on a trained team of volunteers to help the women after the Government funded support at the safe house. It has proved an invaluable resource for the women in community.

In October 2014 I was invited to Romania again, to speak at an international conference regarding victim care provisions in the UK. It was refreshing to see European countries starting to work together to put the needs of the survivor at the heart of actions. There were representations from many NGOs and anti-trafficking police teams throughout the world, and the dedication and commitment of individuals and organizations was inspiring.

During my time in Romania I took the opportunity to visit a woman who had left the safe house and was now being cared for by a NGO in her own country. It was wonderful to see that she was thriving and had the care she needed to build a great future, away from the risk of re-trafficking. She was thrilled to see me, and the knowledge that she had not been forgotten was such a comfort to her.

In November 2014 I left my role at the safe house. After many years dedicated to caring for survivors of human trafficking, I decided to devote more of my time to my own growing family. I have recently been blessed with two beautiful granddaughters, who are a joy to me and my extremely tolerant husband.

Following long and unsociable hours at the safe house I now continue my fight to see the end of modern-day slavery in the UK. I have a lifelong passion to see ongoing support of survivors especially now following the 45-day government-funded provision. I had the honor of becoming a trustee of the Snowdrop Project. I have the time now to devote to numerous women's projects which help not only former victims of trafficking but also many vulnerable women and girls at risk.

I have ongoing involvement in projects with various organizations and an advisory group. I have retained strong links with NGOs in Romania and plan another trip again this year. I will always continue to keep in touch with many of the women and it is a comfort to know where many are now. Some women, even after many years still struggle with mental health issues, and depression, but thankfully they are still surrounded by people who care. Others have received education and vocational training, gaining good careers and prospects. Some are happily married with families of their own.

With the love, care and commitment it is more than possible for survivors to live fulfilled and happy lives. I will continue to make myself available to help make a difference to the amazing women who have suffered in most horrific circumstances. The best is yet to come!

Tina English is a trustee and caseworker for The Snowdrop Project. Over the years she has found she's been given many opportunities to help and work with survivors of human trafficking and has found it a joy and a privilege to witness many journeys of recovery and restoration. She continues her personal fight to see an end to human slavery in her lifetime. To find out more about the work being done to support victims of trafficking visit www.snowdropproject.co.uk.

Chapter 15
My Justice Journey
Danielle Strickland

I was trying to get my 3-year-old to take some medicine to treat an ear infection. He wasn't interested. 'No way,' he said, shaking his head and closing his mouth. I even had banana-flavored liquid penicillin and an easy applicator for the occasion. My eldest son and I acted like monkeys in the hope that our little drama might encourage him, but to no avail: there was no way he was going to take it.

I eventually resorted to what many parents have done around the world . . . I held him down and administered the necessary dose while he tried to resist. 'Yes way,' I said as I shoved the medicine down his throat. In that moment, God spoke to me.

He told me that I do salvation like I did medicine. I shove a little banana-flavored dose of personal relief to people whether they like it or not. 'Yes way,' I say about personal salvation. After all, sin is a disease you can die from, so we don't want to fool around. If we don't get the remedy into individual lives, they will die.

It is true that sin will kill us. Death is the inevitable result of a disease killing us all from the inside out. The gospel is a remedy indeed – and as we receive Jesus into our lives, he acts like a medicine treating our deepest and most horrible human condition. But salvation is bigger than just a remedy for individual sin. It's larger than a personal salvation.

This large vision was what God invited me into. He reminded me of the founders of the Salvation Army, a militant group of ragtag disciples, with a mission to redeem the earth and banish wickedness. William Booth had a vision of a vast ocean of love lapping at the shores of all of humanity just waiting to redeem the entire earth. It was massive. It was epic.

He went on to flesh it all out in a social scheme called *In Darkest England and the Way Out*. It included things like recycling, jobs for the poor, the creation of colonies in new worlds and basic ideas for a new social order founded on equality. It was amazing. To call it large would be, well, an understatement.

The Holy Spirit helped me realize in that moment that I had missed some essential things about the nature of the gospel. Sure, it is a personal remedy. But it is much more than that.

We use that most familiar passage of scripture, John 3:16, the 'God so loved the world that he gave his only son' verse, to explain the gospel. Now some Christians substitute a person's name for that word 'world' – and that pretty much epitomizes how we keep making the vision smaller.

But in the original text that word actually means 'cosmos.' In other words, Jesus came to love and redeem the whole created order. His coming to earth was an unequivocal manifesto of redemption for the entire cosmos.

Paul says later in Romans that the entire creation 'groans' for redemption. This longing to be redeemed is at the heart of all of us. Booth explained in his vision that salvation is only really established if a person's character changes (inside out) and his conditions change (outside in).

This revelation saved me from too small a salvation. And it rescued me from a personal faith that denies the redemption of all of humanity in the equation of love God has for the world. It's not enough to lead someone to a personal relationship with Jesus if they are still bought and sold to the highest bidder. It's not enough to just pray for the poor when they are still dying from extreme poverty.

Salvation's work is personal and public. It's a re-establishing of God's intentions for the entire created order.

I mention that revelation because without it, all our attempts at change are futile on both sides. I can rescue a woman from a brothel but cannot bring about forgiveness or heal her soul. Both need to happen, but only God can work that kind of redemption.

My journey with justice happened as I made friends with people who were socially excluded. As I became friends with people who suffered from exploitation, I began to be bothered by their condition. It wasn't just a terrible thing that happened – it was happening to someone I loved and it became intolerable. I had to intervene. I had to do something to help.

As I tried to help one person at a time out of exploitation, I soon noticed a pattern emerging. This wasn't just a personal issue, it was systemic. That led me to find out the patterns of injustice against certain groups of people and start challenging the laws, protection, housing, provision and societal norms that made this kind of thing happen over and over again.

This is justice: the restoration of wrong, the ending of systemic violence, the re-establishment of norms and standards in society. Here are some things that help us on the journey:

Choose to see

My perspective changed when I moved in with people who were socially excluded to try and see life from their perspective. This shifted a lot of things in me. Suddenly I could feel the weight of injustice against them – the attitudes and prejudices that kept society at arm's length, the exclusion they suffered and what caused their systemic exploitation. I could no longer choose to ignore what was right in front of me.

For example, the east-side of Vancouver, Canada's poorest postal code, is filled with drug-users and people with mental illness and infectious diseases. If you are visiting downtown Vancouver, and get a walking map of the city from the tourist office, the eastside is concealed under the legend. You cannot even see the street names of the neighborhood. The message is clear – we do not want you to see this.

Make friends

If you find yourself lacking empathy, if you end up being appalled by human suffering but not enough to move you off your couch and get your hands dirty, then this step is a key. Go and find some socially excluded people to love, and it will help you to see.

Our society is designed around sameness: we like to hang out and are most comfortable with people who are like us. Finding people who aren't like us is difficult but important. The best way to do this is to hang out in places of social exclusion and make some new friends. As you break down barriers in your own lives, it will teach you about the larger issues that need to be addressed for reconciliation to thrive.

Pray

A few years ago I moved to a community of faith in a low-income neighborhood. We had no funding and no idea what to do, so we did the one thing we knew would help for sure – we prayed.

Now, people may think that prayer is passive but if you understand what God is like, you will know that this move is very strategic. We started to pray specifically for women who were being sexually exploited on the streets around us. About three months into a non-stop prayer room, a man knocked on our door with the keys to an outreach van and a yearly grant to help women get off the street.

I'm not making this up. It became very clear that this was part of God's plan for mobilizing us. He takes great delight in including and empowering the poor and the weak and the lost. We took the hint and the help and started a ministry that just keeps expanding in depth and reach. Prayer is a serious strategy in the fight for justice.

Work hard

I've never been part of a social justice strategy, or mission implementation that was easy. It has been fun, exhilarating, full, dramatic and many other things but never easy. Justice is hard work because it is defying the established order, it is risky and it causes offence.

It takes commitment to really make a difference in the world. Sometimes I meet people who had amazing dreams of a better world but when they set off to try and do something, it got difficult. They figured this meant that they got the message wrong, so they packed it in and did something else.

I'm telling you right now that it will be hard and that we need to grow muscles and stamina for the long fight that lies ahead. Justice goes against the grain of sin, depravity and established social systems . . . it means swimming against the tide and learning to do things differently.

Our street van goes out in the cold at night and into the early hours of the morning to be available to women who need it. Many women don't seem to want help right away, and some are even abusive. It doesn't pay anything, and some nights you feel as if you are wasting your precious time. But that's what justice feels like. It feels like hard work.

Community

This step naturally follows the last one: because this work is hard, it requires more than our individual capacity. We cannot do this stuff alone; we weren't designed to. There is no such thing as a justice superhero; there are communities committed to change together. We must find like-minded and motivated people to accompany us.

Some have journeyed this way before, so we need to seek their advice and maybe even join in with their movement before trying to start our own. It's hard to wait when you are ready to attack evil and rush into doing good, but people who have been about this work for a while know some important things. Becoming a learner and working in community is a strategy for success.

Celebrate

Some of the most amazing social transformers were people of great joy. The work of justice can be long, hard and discouraging. Having a vision that includes redemption for the entire world can make our everyday advances seem small and insignificant. But we serve a God who rejoices when he finds and saves one lost sheep, so we take nothing for granted.

In our communities we try to celebrate every bit of good news as if it's the best news. We aren't operating out of fear or cynicism, because we know that God is on the side of justice and that in the end justice is going to win.

Recently we held a 'year free' party for a woman who had gotten out of sexual exploitation one year ago. It included karaoke and party hats, loads of food and tons of fun. It was a celebration of what one life means, a recognition of hard work and community, and a symbol of hope for every woman who is still on the streets but with the capacity for change. It looked like the kind of justice that is good news to the poor, and is infectiously fun to be part of.

Want to join me?

My experience with Jesus has taken me to streets and alleys where I've seen the deep darkness of injustice and sin, and to city halls and parliaments advocating for new legislation to protect the poor, where I've seen apathy and indifference. I have also witnessed again and again the goodness and kindness of God expressed through presence, community and advocacy.

There is no end to the kind of redemption God has in mind for this earth – the scriptures suggest we couldn't even comprehend it. So, we work and love with this vision in mind, our eyes fixed on a coming Kingdom that will bring heaven to earth.

I once asked a social reformer what is needed to change the world. She said that the first thing is to imagine a better world. This isn't so hard for those of us who know Jesus: he spells out a world that doesn't harm or hurt, that isn't divided by race or gender or class, that loves and gives rather than takes and harms. It's his kingdom, and that's what we keep our eyes on.

The second requirement is to understand oppression. To really get to root issues of social injustice will require what Jesus modeled – 'incarnation.' We must be willing to get our hands and lives dirty and find the secret places of weakness, for systems of injustice to be toppled. This is being heavenly minded while doing earthly good.

I'm praying for generations to be committed to making this Kingdom of God come, to bringing justice on the earth. Like the Psalmist, I declare that I will see the goodness of God in the land of the living. Want to join me?

Danielle Strickland is a Major in The Salvation Army, based in Canada. Danielle has chosen to do grassroots life intentionally in and with marginalized communities around the world. Passionate about dignity and equality for women, she has established ministries to see people freed from prostitution, chaplain teams that visit brothels and massage parlors in three countries, and led the Australian and Canadian chapters of the global campaign Stop The Traffik. From governments to conferences, Danielle advocates and speaks in order to mobilize people to live a life towards justice. Isaiah 58 makes her heart beat faster.

http://www.daniellestrickland.com/

Chapter 16
Aware and Convinced, Compassionate and Collaborative
Bishop Pat Lynch

[From his address in Rome in March 2014
at the Practical Academy of Sciences.]

I would like describe how I personally have become more aware of the tragedy of human trafficking, and how I have become more committed to doing what I can to eliminate it. I will summarize that journey in four simple phrases: becoming aware, becoming convinced, being compassionate and being collaborative.

Becoming aware

About three years ago the Catholic Church in England and Wales held a conference on human trafficking in London, in partnership with the Metropolitan Police. About fifty people attended, representing different dioceses, religious orders and organizations involved in combating this evil.

Inspector Kevin Hyland spoke on the extent of human trafficking in the UK, giving examples from his own experience. Afterwards he was contacted by a representative from the Embassy of the

Philippines who disclosed that she and her colleagues were aware of about sixty young Filipino women who had been trafficked or exploited in the UK by just one criminal gang.

For me, that was a very powerful wake-up call. Whilst I was aware that human trafficking was a serious problem in the world, I did not realize the extent that it occurred in the city where I live – London. It also helped me to realize the important role the Church could play in giving people confidence to trust the law enforcement agencies, especially when the victims concerned were undocumented migrants.

So the first step for me (and indeed for all of us) is to become more aware of the extent of human trafficking and the terrible suffering it causes, and more aware that it may well be happening in our city and in our diocese, in our town or in our parish.

Becoming convinced

Surely all of us are totally convinced about the importance of responding to the scourge of human trafficking in the world today – or are we? In his recent letter Pope Francis in forceful language asks, 'Where is your brother and sister who is enslaved? Where is the brother and sister whom you are killing each day in clandestine warehouses, in rings of prostitution, in children used for begging, in exploiting undocumented labor? Let us not look the other way.'

Certainly we bishops could not get clearer leadership, convincing us of the priority of working to combat human trafficking for our mission and for the common good. However, it is my experience that in many places there is still a lack of awareness about the reality and extent of human trafficking. There is also a lack of conviction and commitment to take collective action to combat it.

Being compassionate

Last September I had the opportunity to visit Nigeria and the privilege of seeing how the Church, particularly the religious orders of women, is responding to human trafficking there. It was truly inspiring to hear the stories of the sisters' courage as they go out to the borders to rescue victims and to hear of the wonderful care they provide for survivors.

This tremendous work is being replicated by religious orders of women throughout the world today – in Africa and Asia, in Latin America and London, in Eastern and Western Europe. Their contribution deserves wholehearted acknowledgement and support from both governments and the Church. Your care for those who suffer the most is a tremendous witness to the compassion of Christ in the world today.

Being collaborative

I have certainly learnt in the last two years that the only way we can confront the scourge of human trafficking and slavery in the world today is by working together. It is important that Church organizations work with law enforcement agencies, and that statutory bodies work with voluntary bodies.

The Catholic Church with its worldwide structure of Episcopal Conferences and enormous network of charitable agencies spread throughout Asia, Africa, Australia, Latin America, Eastern and Western Europe is particularly well placed to play a key role in helping to build an effective global network to combat human trafficking.

This is a journey we – the Catholic Bishops in England and Wales – know we have to make if we are to respond as effectively as we can to those who are suffering. We need to create the good will and establish the networks to enable this to happen everywhere.

Josephine Bakhita

I'd like to finish with the inspiring story of a courageous woman called Josephine Bakhita who at the age of nine was kidnapped, sold and subsequently re-sold into slavery several times in her native Sudan. She suffered so terribly at the hands of her kidnappers that she forgot her birth name. Her kidnappers gave her the name 'Bakhita' which means 'Fortunate.'

Finally, the Italian Consul rescued her and brought her to Italy where she was entrusted to the care of the Canossian Sisters in Venice. It was there she came to know and experience God's love.

Josephine became a Catholic in 1890 and made her final profession in the order in 1896. For the next fifty years she led a life of simplicity, prayer and service as the doorkeeper in the convent, always showing kindness to everyone especially the children in the street.

In her final years she suffered from sickness and the haunting memories of the beatings and flogging she received whilst in slavery. She died in 1947 and was canonized as a saint in October 2000. Her suffering is a reminder of the enduring tragedy of slavery; her courage and sanctity a reminder of the enduring power of the human spirit and indeed of God's grace.

Bishop Pat Lynch is a bishop in the Archdiocese of Southwark, London, with responsibility for the south east pastoral area. He also oversees the Roman Catholic Church's response to human trafficking in the UK.

Chapter 17
Trafficking in Human Persons: A Joined-Up Response
Sister Imelda Poole, IBVM (Loreto)

Alda was kidnapped when she was 16 years old. They had tried to separate her from the other people in the village. She knew one of the traffickers and begged not to be taken away. She arrived home deeply distressed. Next day the traffickers came, fetched her from her home and sold her on to someone else. Her family searched for many months, but, when they found her, it was too late. Tragically, she had hanged herself. The traffickers were never found. **Karina** was sold outside her own country. When she was able to escape the traffickers and return home, her family did not want to see her in the house or in the village. They said she would diminish the authority of the family. A **young woman** I know reports several stories of trafficking which happened in the city where she studied. The men attracted girls who were living in poverty with their beautiful cars and then they trafficked them.

Who are these people and why is it happening? People like Alda and Karina are seeking better lives and are vulnerable to the lies and traps of migrant smugglers and human traffickers. They are from families in poverty where abuse, rejection and abandonment are the stuff of life.

Victims of human trafficking can be men or boys, women, young girls and children. Profiles of victims include the educated and the uneducated, but the one factor common to all is their vulnerability. Let us not look the other way. There is greater complicity than we think. The issue involves everyone!

The global reality today is that millions are being made captives of this modern-day slavery. What are these conditions leading to this phenomenon? How do our cultures and corporate systems create this vulnerability?

We see many causes: the lack of social safety nets, dysfunctional families with violence and neglect, economic poverty, patriarchal cultures, political instability/war zones, natural disasters, criminal activity, illegal immigration status, and lack of education. The men and women engaged in this crime are driven by the need for power and control, the greed for easy money, and the influence of consumerism.

Sisters of the Institute of the Blessed Virgin Mary (Loreto), a religious congregation founded by Mary Ward in 1609, came to Albania in 2005. They sought to respond to a great need with the gifts of the charism of Mary Ward, freedom, justice and sincerity. Ways were sought to minister amongst the most vulnerable to being trafficked and the victims of trafficking. This was undertaken as a mission of God and IBVM Loreto are supporting it in collaboration with many young Albanian professionals.

Albania's challenges

A UNESCO Report in 2013 states:

> Albania still ranks as one of the poorest countries in Europe, facing issues with high unemployment,

widespread corruption, a dilapidated physical infrastructure, powerful organized crime networks, and combative political opponents. Pressing problems, including poverty and stark gender disparities, threaten the economic health of the country and its residents.

The agricultural sector which accounts for almost half of employment but only about one fifth of GDP is limited primarily to small family operations and subsistence farming because of lack of modern equipment, unclear property rights, and the prevalence of small, inefficient plots of land. Albania continues to be an import-oriented economy and, despite reforms, its export base remains small, narrow and undiversified.

Mary Ward Loreto and partnerships

Mary Ward Loreto (MWL) is a non-government organization founded to work against trafficking in Albania. At the heart of its philosophy is a desire to work in partnership and in the belief that all co-workers are leaders within their particular spheres of expertise and responsibility. All at MWL are young, professional Albanians who are dedicated, have a passion for this work and are excellent in the field.

God is at the very heart of this mission, so the work of God will continue always as we respond to those on the margins, the neglected peoples of our world. All peoples are equal in God's eyes and with God there are no favorites. The essence of the Gospel is inclusivity, and this message gives MWL its direction. The call to live for justice, especially with those must vulnerable and excluded, is a call to walk alongside Christ, carrying the cross with him and with those who are suffering in our world.

When non-profit NGOs such as MWL partner to tackle urgent issues in Albania, they can realize wonderful transformations. With cross-sector cooperation, providing a systemic impact and engaging affected constituencies directly, the problem-solving process achieves excellent results.

Pressing problems, including poverty and stark gender disparities, threaten the economic health of the country and its residents. In the rural areas and informal sectors of the cities, many migrant populations from the mountains in Albania have settled in great poverty. These are the areas in which people are most vulnerable to being trafficked.

Our mission is to effect systemic and cultural change by initiating and developing well-thought-through projects and partnerships which tackle major issues, at grass-roots level. MWL is having a positive impact on the lives of individuals, communities, institutions and policies as well as on attitudes and norms.

We particularly seek to confront trafficking in human persons, gender inequality and exclusion, exclusion and poverty of the ethnic minorities, youth unemployment and the systemic changes in education, which affect everything else.

Trafficking in human persons

MWL has responded to the cry of the vulnerable to being trafficked in Albania through direct action with the victims, in prevention, awareness-raising and in advocacy. We form partnerships and work with several main groups: women in rural regions; children and victims of trafficking; ethnic-minority children; prisoners from nine prisons in the Tirana/Durres diocese; youth and (in the future) men from rural regions.

Our aim is to enhance personal development and to offer a better quality of life to members of local communities, notably people vulnerable to human trafficking. This affirms each person's right to human dignity.

The story below presents the reality of the mission field in Albania today.

My name is Sarisa. I was born in a small village in the north of Albania. I am 25 years old. I went to school from the age of six until I was eighteen. My father wanted me to leave school at fourteen when I had completed the compulsory eight years. However I begged and begged my teachers to speak to him, and he finally agreed that I could carry on to secondary school.

I dreamed of becoming a teacher or a nurse, but my father would not allow it. He told me that a woman does not need an education and that I should stay at home to help my mother who suffered ill health. So from then on I would work around the house and farm, helping with the vegetables and livestock and doing household chores.

I first saw Danni in January 2012. I had not met him before, but when my father sent me shopping I would see him driving backwards and forwards in his car. He always seemed to be looking at me. He was rich and his affection and gifts were so novel and drew me to him. He offered me a way out of my 'prison.' He gave me a phone and we kept in touch. He had a nice car and he took me to his flat; later he offered me a new life in another country.

For six months he showed affection and looked after me. Then one day he did not come back. He had sold me to another trafficker who brutally beat me and made me work for him in the sex trade. It was a life of horror. I became so ill that one day a client, realising my state, enabled me to be set free. I wonder if I will ever get over such a nightmare . . .

Gender Inequality and Exclusion

Mary Ward's Women (MWW), is a project of Mary Ward Loreto which is attempting to address the issues which leave women so vulnerable to being trafficked in Albania. It is common for men (husbands) to lose their job or be unable to access work because of the worsening economic crisis in Albania. The responsibility to provide an income now partly falls on the women, who were previously not allowed to take a job.

The deteriorating economic situation leads to serious consequences such as the need to borrow money leading to deep debt, and the need to cover education and health-care costs for the children and the elderly from an empty purse. Strained family dynamics can involve men becoming dependent on home-made alcohol, often leading to domestic violence.

Women's awareness that economic empowerment is a path to independence makes them look for work. MWW helps them prepare for work and for taking new initiatives, as often a long period of unemployment has affected their self-confidence. Also they need to be emotionally prepared to face the objections of their husband or the wider family, or they will avoid facing any debate on this issue and so refuse to look for work.

Domestic violence against women is a growing phenomenon in Albanian rural families. It has been a traditional way of keeping women under control and showing the superiority of men. Women have to deal with violent or drunk husbands, as well as the interference of the husband's family in a couple's relationship or other domestic issues. Women are more exposed to violence when they are asking for any rights in the family.

Violence against children has also traditionally been used, often by parents, to 'educate' them or many times as a way to decompress the adults' own emotional overload. Parents are often volatile and critical of their children, which can lead to more conflict between the couple. Girls are often seen as the chattel of men and married at an early age. The vulnerability this creates exposes children to a lurking trafficker who is calculating to deceive them.

Counseling is offered by the Mary Ward's Women project to respond to this cry and help women and girls overcome their trauma. Women are often more aware of their emotional state and the importance of psychological support. They present with many issues such as stress, depression, trauma, anxiety, and relationship problems. The needs to be addressed are those identified by the women.

Today this project works in eight rural or informal regions of Albania with strong women's groups, empowered by social psychologists and leaders from the groups, chosen by the women themselves. Individual and group counseling is offered and also human development, health-care and health-prevention programs.

As the women become stronger and recognize their own worth they begin to set up social businesses in the regions. So far these businesses include the cultivation of flowers, beans and sage, hand-made card-making, jewelry, and pyrography. All of these goods have a ready market either in Albania or the UK.

These women are being trained in leadership and positive parenting. They hold their heads up high and know their worth. Many of the men in their lives are now proud of them and family life is being changed little by little. It is already making a small difference in a few places, but hopefully the methodology will be passed on, and more and more women from these vulnerable regions will find their rightful place in society.

Exclusion and poverty of the ethnic minorities

In Albania, the Roma people are the most rejected and despised of people and perhaps the most vulnerable to being trafficked. They have a history of being used as slaves and soldiers in war over thousands of years. After these years of abuse they were taken from India and settled in Eastern Europe.

From the day they are born, the children are used for work, begging on the streets with their mothers. As soon as they can walk they beg on their own, with a watchful eye from afar to ensure the money is given and kept. When a little older, they collect plastics and metal from the street bins for recycling, or they wash car windows, often scoffed at and left with no money for their labor. It is a life of indignity and real abuse.

You could say that all of these children are being trafficked and are our lost children. They live in makeshift tents with no running water or electricity, cold in the winter and very hot in the summer. Such a Roma camp, just five minutes from my apartment in Tirana, changed my life in Albania.

None of the people in the camp had been to school for three generations. Many were not registered as citizens and all suffered from some form of malnutrition. In partnership with the NGO called SHKEJ (Education for Life), and funding from many sources, the Little Angels Centre for early education now supports up to fifty children. Two meals a day are served and most children are registered in a state school and are supported in their education back at the Centre.

The Centre employs Albanian teachers, social workers, a doctor and a psychologist. Through outreach to the camps where the families live in dire poverty and degradation, new life and hope is being offered. The community welcomes this new opportunity.

Much more is needed to ensure that the government and all statutory systems realize their role in bringing dignity to a Roma population who are citizens of Albania but who are treated as unwanted foreigners. Unjust treatment of ethnic minority populations is perhaps one of the key issues that all countries need to confront. They need to ensure that these peoples are no longer vulnerable to being sold to traffickers or indeed to become traffickers themselves as a way out of such poverty and indignity.

Youth and youth unemployment

A group in Albania particularly vulnerable to being trafficked are the youth. Recently, the head of the IMF, Christine Lagarde, spoke at the Guildhall in London of moving into a new global reality. Economic growth, she said, can only come from a stance of inclusivity, where the rich include the poor and offer openings for a renewed role for women at every level of society, especially in the levels of decision making. Growth does not come from exclusion.

She stated,

> Right now, the young countries are seeing a 'youth bulge,' with almost three billion people—half the global population—under 25. This could prove a boon or a bane, a demographic dividend or a demographic time-bomb. A youthful population is certainly fertile ground for innovation, dynamism, and creativity. Yet everything will depend on generating enough jobs to satisfy the aspirations of the rising generation. This calls for a single-minded focus on improving education – and, in particular, on the potentially massive effects of technological change on employment.

> (Richard Dimbleby Lecture, Guildhall, January, 2014).

If these words were heeded, they would lead to huge change in Albania where 60% of the population are under 35 years of age. Many young people are trafficked from or within Albania, because they have lost hope of any opportunities in the country and fall prey to offers from criminals who only want to use them for their own means. They are offered work, marriage, a chance to see the world and, more than anything, some kind of security, relieving them of fear and anxiety.

MWL has launched a new project called Youth Education for Prosperity (YEP) to help respond to these needs. The goal of this youth project is to create life-changing opportunities for every young person. The staff will be working hard to build resilience, promote inclusion and ultimately empower them to overcome their disadvantages.

This Youth Project will hopefully provide a broad range of services designed to tackle vulnerability to being trafficked, homelessness and drug and alcohol issues. It will include health and education programs, community outreach and employment.

The employment service will take a holistic approach and address both personal and vocation issues. It aims to provide tailor-made support and training in order to secure an independent future through meaningful, sustainable employment. The project will provide wrap-around services for young people experiencing multiple and complex issues which create barriers to finding work.

Outreach services will address lack of transport, motivation and engagement, and enable each young person to access support within their own environment and the maximum opportunities. Youth need to feel included, affirmed and empowered to do the work they were born to do and to become the people they dreamed of becoming.

This is the call of Christ in the gospel, to *set the downtrodden free*. This project began in March 2014 and already 300 youth have been interviewed in Albania and their voices are being heard. There is hope for the future.

Systemic changes and awareness raising

The main challenge faced by those of us who work against this form of slavery today is to confront unethical behavior and cultural values. There is a need to work at societal change so that those on the margins of society, are included and empowered, experience self-esteem, are aware of their human dignity and know their human rights. Society has broken down when it does not protect its most vulnerable members.

Awareness-raising against trafficking is seen as an important component of the work of Mary Ward Loreto. As part of United Religious Against Trafficking (URAT), the work began in this field in 2010 with a campaign against trafficking. The members were trained about using social media for campaigning, and studied its risks in promoting the work of the traffickers and its potential for reporting abuse and for education.

Once funding was realized, Mary Ward Loreto was able to employ a member of the group to develop a project in forty vulnerable regions of the country, using a variety of methodologies to help communities to face this crime happening in their midst. Many stories of trafficking have emerged during these trainings, and many tears have been shed.

The work is being done in partnership with the NGO 'Different and Equal' who run a shelter for trafficked victims. We have also partnered with them to fund and work in an education and rehabilitation center for trafficked victims. One of the experienced Different and Equal social workers has been seconded to work alongside the paid MWL social worker in this project. Peace Corps have also partnered with us, with all the organizations sharing their resources for the training programs and helping to gather communities together.

In Albanian culture, it is not acceptable to speak about family problems. Trafficked girls are often stigmatized as prostitutes rather than being regarded as innocent victims, and there is a high level of shame and guilt in the family. A mother tends to take the blame if her daughter does something that is socially unacceptable, including being trafficked. This stigma means that there can be a wall of silence until great trust is built.

Using media such as photo-novella, presenting true stories of trafficking in Albania, has helped to break down this stigma. The methodology used by MWL/URAT also shows the potential traffickers the evil being perpetrated and that they will not necessarily escape severe punishment for their crime.

Our link with the international network of religious against trafficking called Talitha Kum highlighted the need for a European network against trafficking, so Religious in Europe Networking Against Trafficking and Exploitation (RENATE) was founded. Religious from nineteen European countries work across borders together in direct action to protect the victims, give safe shelter, and run various forms of rehabilitation programs.

This network seeks to effect change through a joined-up response to awareness-raising, prevention, advocacy and campaigning. It highlights issues. We have rebuilt the website www.renate-europe.net for greater collaboration and sharing of resources. Social media is vital for campaigning, and its risks for cyber grooming, sexting and bullying must be highlighted.

For religious, it is the work of God to walk alongside the victim and to expose evil. Nothing can stop us from seeking justice in action. We desire more than anything to reveal the truth to those who have been trapped through the deceit of their traffickers.

The words of Pope Francis state this truth:

> Human trafficking is an open wound of contemporary society, a scourge upon the body of Christ. It is a crime against humanity. (April 2014 Conference at the Vatican Against Trafficking.)
>
> I have always been distressed at the lot of those who are victims of various kinds of human trafficking. How I wish that all of us would hear God's cry: 'Where is your brother?' (Genesis 4:9). Where is your brother or sister who is enslaved? Where is the brother and sister whom you are killing each day in clandestine warehouses, in rings of prostitution, in children used for begging, in exploiting undocumented labor.

Let us not look the other way. There is greater complicity than we think. The issue involves everyone! This infamous network of crime is now well established in our cities, and many people have blood on their hands as a result of their comfortable and silent complicity. (Evangelii Gaudium, No 211 2013)

Speaking personally, as I work with these projects I experience God directing me and nudging me on in so many difficult situations. The power and love of God is a passion in my heart which gives courage and picks me up in failure and when things seem too hard. I see God working in the world drawing us into humility, into dependence on God who is the director and guide of all.

Imelda Poole IBVM (Loreto) has been working in the field of anti-trafficking across Europe, for ten years, through the work of the Foundation RENATE and in particular in Albania, through the work of the Foundation, Mary Ward Loreto. This work has challenged Imelda to cross borders in the pursuit of justice and to forge more and more networking links to combat this clandestine and most lucrative crime taking place in our modern world.

www.albaniahope.com

Chapter 18
Crime Stoppers
and Human Trafficking in the US
John Lamb

Truly, I say to you, as you did it to one of the least of these
my brothers, you did it to me.
(Matthew 25:40)

Human Trafficking is a global disease that has plagued many
lives. No country is out of reach from human traffickers; even the
most powerful and secure countries succumb to this infection. Yet
sometimes people are so caught up with their lives that the thought
of others being coerced to sexual or labor slavery never crosses
their minds.

The US Department of Justice reports that 300,000 children are
at risk of being prostituted in the United States. These innocent
children are forced to endure sexual intercourse up to 20-40 times
a day, according to the Polaris Project. According the United Nations,
human trafficking generates $9.5 billion annually in the United States.

Someone has to look out for these victims; someone must be the
Earth's immune system against traffickers who worship nothing but

the smell of a dollar. Someone should act as God's hand here on earth to deliver these victims from their ordeal. Enter Crime Stoppers USA.

Crime Stoppers USA is an organization led by citizens against crime and its mission is to be the premier community-based crime-solving programme in the United States. The organization was a brainchild of a young Albuquerque detective who was frustrated that leads on the murder of a college student had been exhausted.

The detective felt that relevant information was available from someone other than the criminal. This led to the coming together of the local community, media and law enforcement, giving birth to the first Crime Stoppers program. After the media publicized the case, an informant came forward leading to the arrest of three men.

Today, Crime Stoppers program reach around the world, encouraging people with information about a crime to share their knowledge in exchange for a cash reward while ensuring anonymity. Crime Stoppers USA has enjoyed a tremendous amount of success with an average conviction rate of 95% on cases addressed by its system. Currently, Crime Stoppers USA is working with different organizations to try to stop the terrible harm of human trafficking.

Crime Stoppers working against trafficking

One of CSUSA's most ambitious projects is the development and creation of a national education course to assist law enforcement in understanding what human trafficking is and recognizing its telltale signs. For example, at the 2014 Training Conference at Austin Texas, Crime Stoppers educated law enforcement officers on subjects such as how to properly use tip-offs, how to deal with law enforcement coordinators and the different duties of a coordinator.

Training on how to identify and recognize signs of human trafficking is crucial to rescuing victims. In Halton, police officers rescued an 18-year-old woman who was allegedly being exploited.

They had received a significant amount of funding for a special investigation targeting the sex trade, surveillance and officer training against trafficking.

In New Jersey, police saved a 26-year-old woman after she was ordered to make money through the sex trade or suffer the consequences at the hands of her perpetrators. In the Gloucester Township police report, Acting Attorney General Hoffman stated, 'When a young woman is transported into this state and sells herself for sex because of threats and intimidation, she is a sexual slave, not a prostitute.' Prior to this case, the town's police force participated in training sessions about human trafficking cases for nearly a year. These sessions have certainly born fruit for the 26-year-old woman.

Cases like these highlight the need for law enforcement training on identification and recognition of human trafficking. However, CSUSA doesn't stop at working with law enforcement to check modern-day slavery. The organization is championed by ordinary citizens who have the courage to make a call in order to save the life of an unsuspecting victim. CSUSA is committed to educate the public on recognition of possible human trafficking cases.

Most of the time, Americans believe that human trafficking only occurs in developing countries. In Wist TV's report, Reggie Lloyd stated, 'Most people don't believe that this is going on, most people have never seen it, never heard of it, so it makes it very difficult for them as average citizens to take a look at a situation and say, "You know, this could be a human trafficking case."' At the time, Lloyd was prosecuting the first case of human trafficking in South Carolina in which a 14-year-old girl was trafficked to a pimp and forced to serve dozens of men a day.

Spotting the signs

With the creation of a national education course for the public, Crime Stoppers USA hopes more and more people will phone law enforcement to give anonymous tips about possible cases of forced labor or sexual slavery. The 'Read Between the Lines' campaign challenges the public to report signs such as:

- Presence of heavy security in the premises
- Barred windows, locked doors, or electronic surveillance
- People living in cramped conditions
- People living and working at the same address
- Workers being driven back and forth between premises
- Workers wearing inappropriate clothing and lacking safety equipment
- Workers being collected early and driven back late at night
- Workers showing signs of injury, malnourishment, and unkempt appearance
- Workers isolated from the rest of the community

Anyone with information on human trafficking, no matter how insignificant it may seem, is encouraged to call and take action as Crime Stoppers believes that any information may lead to the deliverance of a poor soul.

An anonymous tip saved a 15-year-old girl from the clutches of her tormentors who had brought her from Los Angeles to Oxnard for the purpose of child prostitution. Her case is only one of many thousands of human trafficking crimes happening throughout the US on a daily basis.

It is definitely happening on American soil, and it's time for the public to awaken to this issue. Someone has to be on a lookout for these incidents, and CSUSA is hoping that that someone is the one reading this book.

Aside from working with police and the public, CSUSA is also working with the Polaris Project in Washington DC, an organization at the forefront of ending the scourge of human trafficking. It offers many services that can be beneficial to our members like training and technical assistance, fellowship programs, and global programs.

At the 2014 Crime Stoppers USA Conference, the Polaris Project played a key role, showing how important local efforts can be in eliminating human trafficking and how Crime Stoppers can help. The conference also covered:

- Establishing connection and working with local US Marshals' offices
- Raising program awareness
- Connecting and maintaining vital relationships with the media
- Campus Crime Stoppers for students
- How the program can fight the heinous crime of human trafficking
- Enhanced rewards for some cases

Airline Ambassadors against trafficking

In the crusade against modern-day slavery we have also started working with Airline Ambassadors International, the flight attendants group founded by Nancy Rivard. This charity began as a group of flight attendants wanting to use their pass privileges to help others. The organization escorts children who require assistance, hand-delivers humanitarian aid and educates people on child protection.

AAI decided to get involved in the fight against human trafficking in 2009 when they rescued an abandoned little girl in Cambodia. On the way back to the US, the flight attendants involved identified four incidents of trafficking. Since then, AAI has worked with organizations in both the public and private sectors to combat human trafficking. The idea is to have airline personnel watching out for signs of victims being transported across international borders.

An example of human trafficking via airline travel was reported by the official website of the city of New York. Alena P. was a Russian performer in Russia who came to the United States under the impression that she would work for a theatre troupe. However, upon arrival, her passport was confiscated and she was physically threatened. Her perpetrators told her that she would have to work to pay off the debt she accrued for travelling to the US. She had to work for a whole year until the day that one of her roommates escaped and reported the case to the police, which led to her freedom and the arrest of her traffickers.

To stem the growing number of people being sold to sexual and labor slavery every day, CSUSA is in discussions with AAI about helping international flight attendants to report potential human trafficking cases securely. To further ensure that the report remains anonymous, Crime Stoppers is also working with the Department of Homeland Security.

It is important that anyone who is on a flight and notices something suspicious about a specific passenger or group of passengers, doesn't hesitate to speak with the attendant in private about the issue. Rest assured that there are organizations who will listen with a sense of urgency.

Trafficking in Oklahoma

Most Americans do not believe that sex trafficking and slave labor might be happening across the street. Surprisingly, Oklahoma is one of the worst states in the USA for labor and sex trafficking. According to Enid News, Oklahoma City is problematic because of its location in the crossroads of the country and the number of truck stops in the state.

Mark Elam, executive director of Oklahomans against Trafficking Humans, reports, 'In the last six weeks, we have had over 200 truckers calling and reporting young girls at a truck stop or rest stop area.' Countless victims pass through Oklahoma every day and most people are clueless about what's happening.

Another factor why Oklahoma is one of the biggest states for human trafficking cases is the state's high divorce rate, as broken or dysfunctional families may result in the child escaping from the problems at home. Running away makes these children vulnerable to trafficking. Elam goes on to say, 'To find poor and uneducated, vulnerable women and children, Oklahoma, Arkansas and Kansas are hot spots in the nation.' Human Trafficking Statistics for Oklahoma reports:

- One child is abducted every 18 minutes.
- More than 2000 children are reported missing each day.
- One child runs away from home every six minutes.

These statistics are from the state of Oklahoma alone and not from the entire country! It is our hope that through the help of ordinary citizens as witnesses, these numbers will be significantly reduced, if not completely eradicated.

In a recent report of human trafficking by Fox23, police arrested a male suspected of trafficking for the purpose of prostitution. A teenage girl was brought from Kansas City, to Tulsa to have sex with men in an inn and the perpetrator kept all the cash she made from her services. The teenage girl was taken to a safe place while the suspect went to jail.

After an undercover sting operation known as Operation Trojan Horse, News on 6 reported that during this four-day crackdown, undercover officers posed as either prostitutes or clients. Men who were expecting to pay for sex and women who were ready to sell their bodies were all taken into custody, resulting to 42 arrests. After interviewing each suspect, law enforcement agents found out that three people were potential victims of sex trafficking, including a 15-year-old girl.

In addition to this case, on July 30, 2013, 60 arrests were made by the FBI in Oklahoma City as reported in News9. The local operation resulted to the rescue of three girls in their mid-teens who were being prostituted.

Gary Johnson of the FBI stated, 'The exploiters target the under-aged girls because it's easier for them to do that than try to exploit a 25-year-old prostitute. It's a lot easier to exploit a 15- or 16-year-old runaway.' Mark Elam said that girls who acted out were beaten as an example in front of other victims. These harrowing incidents further illustrate the need for help, action, and vigilance.

Aside from sex trafficking, Oklahoma is no stranger to labor trafficking, the recruitment of foreigners who are to be coerced to slavery. These individuals are subjected to long working hours in factories, sweatshops, and restaurants with minimal or no compensation, commonly in horrible conditions and under heavy surveillance.

In the report of *The Times of Pryor Creek Oklahoma*, a Tulsa factory closed in 2002 after allegations that the employers lured 52 workers from India and hired them as skilled laborers. However, the victims were subjected to abuse, intimidation, and exploitation. Four years later, a federal judge ordered the owner to pay the victims a hefty $1.3 million. Although justice was served for these victims, more will continue to slave away for the profits of their handlers unless their transgressions are curtailed through the assistance of the public.

Where is God?

With all the cases of human trafficking we know of and millions more that are still undocumented, one might doubt the presence of the Almighty God. Where is God when families are falling apart and children feel the need to run away? Where is God when young women flee abuse only to end up at the hands of new and more evil abusers?

Where is God when thousands children are sold into sexual slavery, and then resold again? Where is God when young girls are beaten in plain sight of other victims? Truly, it is a challenge to be a Christian in a very un-Christian world.

It is only normal to wonder, and asking questions is just another form of prayer. Jesus said, 'Ask and it will be given to you; seek and you will find; knock and the door will be opened to you' (Matthew 7:7).

Many great things have begun from questions, and asking God's presence in the middle of these appalling cases of human trafficking will lead to answers. God has been alive, present, and ever powerful in the stories that have been presented.

I believe God inspired the struggling young Albuquerque detective who founded Crime Stoppers because he was intent on solving a case. God worked in the hearts of people in media who cared enough to publicize the case, and God in the life of the anonymous person who gave critical information about the case.

He was also present when police officers rescued an 18-year-old woman being prostituted in Halton, North West England, and in the saving of a 26-year-old woman in Gloucester Township, New Jersey. God worked in the deliverance of the 14-year-old girl being forced into sexual slavery in South Carolina. God showed his power when an anonymous tip-off saved a 15-year-old girl from her tormentors' clutches in Oxnard, California, and when the captors of Alena P., the Russian performer, were arrested.

God was also present when the largest human trafficking ring in Canada was shut down, and when police listened to the complaints of two girls in Panama. Even in one of the most problematic states in the US, God's will was shown when more than 40 were arrested and three victims of human trafficking were rescued in a sting operation, and when the 60 were arrested by the FBI and three teenage girls were saved. God's justice was demonstrated to the employer in Tulsa who trafficked 52 Indian laborers.

God is present when organizations come together to address the growing problem of human trafficking. Jesus said, 'For where two or three gather in my name, there am I with them,' (Matthew 18:20). When CSUSA chose to work with law enforcement and the public for the development of a national course about recognition of human trafficking, God was working behind the scenes.

God was also involved when Project Polaris agreed to work with CSUSA and when we collaborated with AAI, and the Department of Homeland Security to stop potential cases of human trafficking. Most importantly, God is present in the lives of people who are coming forward to act and to help.

God is present in the lives of the many readers of this book. Therefore, stay vigilant and have faith. Trust that when the time and situation to act come, God will be everywhere.

John Lamb is the Chairman of Crime Stoppers of the United States of America, Inc., a US-wide network that creates local, community based crime solving programs. Crime Stoppers has developed innovative resources and partnerships to counter crime throughout the US.

http://www.crimestoppersusa.com/

Chapter 19
The US Catholic Bishops'
Fight against Human Trafficking
Bishop Eusebio L. Elizondo

In his apostolic exhortation, our Holy Father speaks to us about human trafficking:

> I have always been distressed at the lot of those who are victims of various kinds of human trafficking. How I wish that all of us would hear God's cry: 'Where is your brother?' (Genesis 4:9). Where is your brother or sister who is enslaved? Where is the brother and sister whom you are killing each day in clandestine warehouses, in rings of prostitution, in children used for begging, in exploiting undocumented labor?
>
> Let us not look the other way. There is greater complicity than we think. The issue involves everyone! This infamous network of crime is now well established in our cities, and many people have blood on their hands as a result of their comfortable and silent complicity.
> *Pope Francis, Evangelii Gaudium, November 2013*

Human trafficking is present in the United States, in brothels, massage parlors, street prostitution, in agriculture, agricultural processing, hospitality – like restaurants, nightclubs, and hotels, in peoples' homes for domestic and personal care, in construction and maintenance and many other industries. Victims can be US citizens or foreign nationals; they can be recruited in the US or trafficked across borders.

Vulnerable migrants

Among foreign national victims, it is often the lack of economic opportunities confronting many communities worldwide that places significant strain on their families. In response, many choose to leave their homes with the hope of making it to the United States, finding worthwhile employment and sending money home. Those who attempt 'irregular migration'[5] risk being caught in the web of human trafficking, where they are compelled into a life of sexual slavery and/or forced labor. Once in the U.S., migrants with irregular status are also vulnerable to exploitation, which can give rise to the severity of human trafficking.

Human trafficking inherently shows contempt for people made in God's image. As the bishops of the United States and Mexico have stated in their pastoral letter *Strangers No Longer*, it 'rejects the dignity of the human person and exploits conditions of global poverty'.[6]

The Church has long been concerned for the most vulnerable. As chair of the United States Conference of Catholic Bishops' Committee on Migration, I believe the Catholic Church cannot rest until trafficking in human persons is eliminated.

---

5. See Perruchoud, R. and Redpath-Cross, J. (eds.) (2011). Glossary on Migration (2nd ed). International Migration Law, no. 25.
6. Catholic Bishops of the United States and Mexico, Strangers No Longer: Together on the Journey of Hope (Washington, DC: USCCB, 2003), no. 90.

The responsibility of the Church

Every Catholic, alongside other persons of good will, can play a part. We are called to educate ourselves and others about human trafficking in order to prevent its occurrence, to build a spirit of hospitality and welcome for survivors of trafficking, and encourage others around us to work at addressing the root causes.

The bishops in the United States, guided by a long tradition of Catholic Social Teaching, have actively engaged a wide range of initiatives to combat the trafficking of human persons, the victims of which are our brothers and sisters in Christ who are subject to the many forms of modern day slavery in our midst.

Such activities include the administration of critical services for survivors, building the capacity of Catholics and others in the United States and abroad to combat trafficking in persons, pastoral statements, and policy and advocacy efforts.

Migration and Refugee Services and anti-trafficking

Many of these initiatives are organized within the Migration and Refugee Services department of the United States Conference of Catholic Bishops (MRS) which works under the direction of the US Bishop's Committee on Migration. Combating human trafficking is a priority of this Committee, in keeping with the worldwide Church and the Holy Father's focus on this issue. MRS has been actively engaged in work of protecting victims of human trafficking for more than a decade.

With a mission rooted in the Catholic teachings of hospitality and the promotion of human dignity, MRS has decades of experience of working with partners nationally in welcoming newcomers to the US and facilitating their integration into their new communities. This includes its long-standing commitment to resettling refugees, serving asylum seekers, and supporting Cuban and Haitian migrants.

Through the programs that MRS administered for these and other migrants, and through communications with sister organizations in the global Church, it became clear that there was a distinct form of abuse and exploitation occurring particularly among migrants, both in the US and abroad. This abuse consists of the organized, deliberate recruitment and control of individuals for their labor in many industries, including the commercial sex industry.

Informed by their extensive work with refugee and asylee populations, MRS recognizes that foreign national victims of trafficking are similar to immigrants in many ways: they need support as they start a new life in a new community, in a new culture.

Victims of trafficking and refugees face similar barriers, including limited English proficiency and an unfamiliarity with US systems, such as schools and other public services. Many victims are undereducated, separated from family members, and have experienced physical and/or mental trauma. In response, Catholic organizations and ministries across the United States have committed themselves to assist survivors of trafficking in a variety of ways, including professional case management, pastoral accompaniment, counseling and legal services.

MRS was among the first round of agencies funded by the federal government to administer national programs for survivors of human trafficking. This was fitting, given that the USCCB was among a small group of organizations with experience serving victims within their existing migration programs. Within a public/private partnership, MRS built a network of over 200 providers over the five-and-a-half year program period, which included Catholic and other faith-based organizations, as well as secular and community-based organizations.

The network providers included a range of service models and expertise: refugee resettlement agencies, domestic violence shelters, immigrant advocacy organizations, and family and community service providers. Through its case management programs MRS provided restorative and lifesaving case management services to more than 3,000 victims of sex and labor trafficking and their eligible family members, including 170 child victims of human trafficking. MRS continues to place unaccompanied foreign child victims of trafficking into refugee foster care programs nationwide.

Several trends emerged during the administration of these services which informed the work of MRS' Anti-Trafficking Office. First, 73% of the clients enrolled in the MRS anti-trafficking program were victims of labor trafficking. This highlighted that this form of trafficking must be a focus of education efforts for law enforcement, social service providers, and the public.

Second, victims in the program originated from 106 different countries. This emphasized the need for attention to diversity in victim identification and service provision, particularly around labor laws. Labor laws, and citizens' expectations of protection, can vary immensely worldwide. All immigrant communities should be empowered to know their rights, and educated about what to do when those rights are violated. Finally, since MRS served victims in more than 200 US locations, it is clear that trafficking occurs in all parts of the United States.

While MRS continues to serve victims through the provision of employment services, in recent years the bishops have re-focused their efforts to prioritize prevention and awareness-raising. This shift in focus was partly due to the recognition that one of the Church's strengths is the fact that we are an 'immigrant church' and have access to the people who are most at risk of becoming victims of trafficking. The emphasis on prevention and awareness-raising initiatives underscores two priorities of the US Conference of Catholic Bishops: affirming the intrinsic value of human life and the dignity of every human being, and embracing the cultural diversity of the Church.

Most human trafficking educational efforts aimed at prevention and awareness-raising target intermediaries (direct social service providers, medical practitioners, law enforcement and other first responders) in order to increase the identification of victims they may encounter in their professional capacities.

Other awareness-raising campaigns, also focused on increasing victim identification, are directed at 'Good Samaritans,' such as students and members of faith-based and civic organizations. While important, these efforts often fail to reach the most vulnerable audiences: the victims of human trafficking themselves, their families, and their communities.

MRS believes that to uphold the dignity of the human person, it is essential that communities most at risk of exploitation are aware of the risks, and are also educated about their rights. This also makes practical sense; while it is true that one tactic used by traffickers is to isolate their victims, in reality many victims (particularly the victims of labor exploitation) are able to maintain some contact with their families and communities. An educated and empowered community is better prepared to protect its most vulnerable members from exploitation, as well as to identify, serve, and pursue justice for members who may have fallen prey to traffickers.

Complicating the situation further, many people being exploited are unaware that they are victims of a specific crime, that self-reporting would prompt an appropriate response, or that there are resources to assist them. Families may inadvertently pressure victims to remain in exploitative situations, hoping that victims' wages will increase or believing that even unjust wages are better than the alternative.

The principle of subsidiarity and 'accompaniment,' which draws on a community's own human resources, is a practical approach to grassroots education and outreach in immigrant communities. MRS tries to leverage the strength of new immigrant communities to build capacity and empower the poor to help themselves. Communities will be educated and empowered to identify victims, create community-based protective responses, and aid in the prevention of future exploitation.

While working in the field of anti-trafficking, MRS observed that survivors choose to live and receive services in communities where they have family and social ties. Family reunification, in which eligible family members are allowed to enter the US to join a survivor, is one of the most meaningful benefits of receiving a T-Visa[7]; but it can be a difficult experience, where unrealistic expectations meet inadequate support or resources.

Similarly, survivors who return to families and their communities face many challenges to overcoming and healing from their exploitation, and starting their lives over. Communities need education on receiving these survivors, and their derivative family members, to ensure they are supported and connected with services and resources to secure a path to self-sufficiency and full reintegration.

MRS is also responsive to the opportunities and challenges presented by changing immigration law. With the prospect of comprehensive immigration reform on the horizon, the relationship between employment and legal immigration status will potentially be strengthened. On the positive side, more visas could be made available for low or unskilled workers, such as hotel employees, landscapers, construction workers, and personal care or domestic workers. However, the dependence that is created between the immigrant, low-skilled worker and their employer opens the possibility of abuse.

In our experience, immigrant workers who rely on their employment for legal status are less likely to complain about unsafe, unjust, or unfair working conditions; are less likely to report

---

7. The T-Visa was established by the TVPA for human trafficking victims. Eligibility requirements include meeting TVPA standards of human trafficking, cooperation with law enforcement efforts if possible (for victims 18+), and proving that deportation would cause "extreme hardship." USCIS source.

harassment, sexual harassment or abuse; and are less likely to file wage and hour violation complaints. Such an environment can lay the groundwork to labor exploitation and human trafficking. Unscrupulous labor recruiters and contractors will no doubt arise to match workers with employers, which can lead to one of the most common and severe forms of human trafficking: debt bondage.

Given the complexity and scope of the problems faced, efforts against human trafficking benefit immensely from educated, empowered communities. The Anti-Trafficking Office of MRS coordinates two educational campaigns: the Amistad Movement and the Become a SHEPHERD Campaign.

The Amistad Movement

The Amistad Movement works with and supports communities nationwide at risk of human trafficking. Relationship-building through the church network has enabled us to develop and encourage local leadership in anti-trafficking education. The initiative uses a community-centered, transformative education approach and relies on a train-the-trainer model that emphasizes coalition-building and leadership within the target communities.

As part of the Amistad Movement, individuals will be trained as Community Educators and reach out to more disenfranchised members of their ethnic communities, in their own languages and through community networks. They will gain skills in community leadership and will be prepared to act as a liaison and representative for their community to existing trafficking coalitions and task forces.

The Community Educators will identify the industries most prevalent in their communities, on which to focus their outreach and educational efforts. In this way, they will become experts on both general and local trafficking issues.

It is a priority to include affected communities in local coalitions and task forces so that any project activities directed to first responders and intermediaries in the project area are informed by community members' experiences. This strategy builds relationships, fosters trust and improves collaboration between community members and anti-trafficking professionals.

The Amistad Movement will increase diversity in diocesan life and leadership. Immigrant community members will be trained to be leaders and representatives, and encouraged to collaborate with other Catholic, other faith-based and secular organizations engaged in anti-human trafficking efforts and related human, labor, and civil rights issues. The project will also create a forum to bring participants together to share their successes, strategies, and challenges.

All components and project materials are rights-based, emphasizing the dignity of the human person and that 'charity begins with justice' (*Caritas in Veritate*). The Amistad Movement prioritizes seeking justice, whether by demanding improved working conditions or through the identification and reporting of human trafficking situations. Participants will be trained about legal protections, how to respond to/report violations, and how to access the resources, services and civil remedies to which victims are entitled.

Become a SHEPHERD

Given the geographic reach of the Catholic Church in the United States that includes countless parish and diocesan leaders who care about issues of human trafficking, MRS prioritizes the development of educational resources for use at the parish level. For example, the 'Become a SHEPHERD' toolkit is available to all parishes interested in learning more about human trafficking.

Individuals can host an educational event at their parish or in their community. The participants learn about the Church's teaching on human trafficking, different forms of human trafficking and exploitation based on real cases, trends in human trafficking cases, how to identify and where to refer victims and those at risk, and how they can contribute to the larger efforts to eradicate human trafficking. Our hope as bishops is that an increasing number of parishes will serve as a meeting place to discuss this issue and be a center for action.

Advocacy by bishops

In addition to their educational initiatives, the bishops have also been closely involved in advocacy efforts in the fight against human trafficking. The US bishops were among the early advocates who worked to define the crime of human trafficking, and to ensure that government legislation and policy addressed the emerging phenomenon.

We have been instrumental in the development and promotion of the Trafficking Victims Protection Act (TVPA) legislation that originally passed in 2000. Using information from the cases that were being uncovered and the individuals being served by the Church, MRS helped define the elements of the crime, and sought to ensure that adequate provisions and protections for victims were included in subsequent renewals of the legislation.

Unique among legal statutes and laws that codify and define criminal acts, the TVPA also defines the social and legal protections available to victims of human trafficking, and ensures their eligibility for services.

Today, the US bishops continue to advocate for legislation which will improve national and international responses to human trafficking. For example, the Bishop's Committee on Migration works with Congress to garner greater prevention, service, and protection mechanisms for possible and identified child labor trafficking victims.

As Chairman, I have written to Congressional members urging their support for legislation which increases information sharing between state child welfare and law enforcement agencies in order to better prevent, identify, and care for child victims of sex trafficking, and to provide for an increase in the identification, protection and service provisions to labor trafficking victims.

Catholics united against trafficking

Recognizing the important role that partnerships play in the fight against slavery, MRS convenes the Coalition of Catholic Organizations Against Human Trafficking. This was originally chartered in 2002 and assembles more than 30 national and international Catholic organizations to eliminate human trafficking through public education, advocacy, and services. The member agencies are independently and collectively organized to protect victims, to prevent an increase in trafficking, and to promote traffickers' prosecution.

From a local to a national level, the coalition members, including many women religious, are raising awareness about the reality of human trafficking across the United States. For example, some members focus on the prevention of human trafficking that often corresponds with major sporting events, while others regularly organize prayer vigils for victims and survivors of human trafficking.

National day of prayer

As part of a global community of faith, Catholics are increasingly praying for the end to the trafficking in persons. In fact, there is a growing movement internationally to further prayer on human trafficking. In autumn 2013, the US Bishops Committee on Migration designated the Feast Day of St. Josephine Bakhita, February 8th, as a national day of prayer for victims and survivors of human trafficking.

St. Josephine spent much of her life under horrible circumstances, until she asserted her humanity and dignity, demanded her freedom and entered the religious life with the Canossian sisters. A victim of human trafficking, St. Josephine was brought from Sudan to Italy and died (free) in 1947. On February 8th, the US bishops encourage parishes to host or attend prayer services and discussion groups, and to reflect on the experiences of those who have suffered through human trafficking and exploitation.

Supporting victims of human trafficking through awareness raising, being a voice in the fight against human trafficking through advocacy efforts on the local and national level and, most importantly, prayer, are the cornerstones of a comprehensive faith-based response to human trafficking. There is so much capacity for us to bring light, to be in solidarity with those affected by human trafficking, and to bring the Gospel into the darkness.

Bishop Eusebio L. Elizondo MSpS is the Auxiliary Bishop of Seattle. He chairs the USCCB Committee on Migration and was invited to attend the first meeting of the President's Advisory Council on Faith-based and Neighborhood Partnerships working day on Human Trafficking, in September 2012.

Chapter 20
Fighting Slavery –
The Irish Government's response
Marion Walsh (Department of Justice and Equality)

I was born and reared in the South West of Ireland, a few miles outside of Listowel in Co. Kerry. From my teenage years I had close exposure to local issues and developed early a sense of what was right, fair and just. I try to apply these values in my personal life and public service work, and they were never as valid and necessary as when dealing with human trafficking.

In February 2008, I was appointed the first Executive Director of Ireland's Department of Justice and Equality's Anti Human Trafficking Unit (AHTU), with the task of developing a coordinated, comprehensive and holistic response to human trafficking. Over four years it was a privilege to work with my colleagues, ministers, other government departments and agencies, international and non-governmental organizations in developing and implementing that response.

Together we were determined to identify and implement effective means to combat human trafficking. This was not just to honor the Irish Government's commitment to comply with international obligations, but also to address this most heinous abuse of human rights. It involved over 540 meetings with relevant stakeholders for the purposes of developing systems, structures and a response.

There is scope for improvements or alterations in the light of international developments and experience gained to date. The response to this complex problem is a work in progress, which continues under my successor, David Gilbride, since he took up the post in March 2012.

The initial Irish response

At the time of my appointment there were already a number of measures in place and others were in train. In addition, funding was (and continues to be) provided by the Department and the Health Services Executive (HSE) to a NGO dealing with sexual exploitation.

Key legislative and administrative measures

Since 1996 the *Sexual Offences (Jurisdiction) Act 1996* has allowed for the prosecution of an Irish citizen, or a person ordinarily resident in Ireland, who commits an act in another country which is a sexual offence against a child. Penalties of up to five years imprisonment apply for persons convicted on indictment.

Since 1998, laws have also been in place relating to sexual exploitation of children. *The Child Trafficking and Pornography Act 1998* makes it an offence to knowingly facilitate the entry into, transit through, or exit from Ireland of a child for the purpose of sexual exploitation or to provide their accommodation for this purpose while in Ireland. The Act also makes it an offence to take, detain or restrict the personal liberty of a child for the purpose of their sexual exploitation, to use a child for such a purpose, or to organize or knowingly facilitate such actions.

In June 2008 the *Criminal Law (Human Trafficking) Act 2008* came into force. That legislation creates an offence of recruiting, transporting, transferring to another person, harboring or causing the entry into, travel within or departure from the State of a person or providing the person with accommodation or employment for the specific purpose of the trafficked person's sexual or labor exploitation, or removal of his or her organs. Penalties of up to life imprisonment apply and, at the discretion of the Court, an unlimited fine.

These penalties also apply for attempting the offences as well as for the sale or offering for sale or purchase or offer to purchase any person. In addition, it is an offence under the Act for a person to solicit for prostitution someone whom there are reasonable grounds for believing is a trafficked person, with penalties of up to five years and/or an unlimited fine.

The Act also amended the 1998 Act by defining a child as a person under the age of 18 years (rather than 17) and raising the penalty from 14 years to life imprisonment.

To protect the identity of suspected victims, there are penalties of up to 10 years imprisonment and/or an unlimited fine for publishing or broadcasting information without judicial consent, which includes photographs or representations of the physical likeness of an alleged victim. The judiciary may now exclude persons – others than those connected with the proceedings – from the court. Alleged victims, with the leave of the court in the case of adults, may give evidence through a live television link, from either within the State or abroad.

In July 2013, the 2008 Act was amended to give full effect to the criminal law measures in the European Union Directive of 2011[8]. The *Criminal Law (Human Trafficking) (Amendment) Act 2013* criminalizes trafficking for the purposes of forced begging or other criminal activities, and defines forced labor. The upper age threshold for out-of-court video recording of a complainant's evidence is increased from 14 to 18 years. Trafficking by a public official during

8. Directive 2011/36/EU of the European Parliament and of the Council on preventing and combating trafficking in human beings and protecting its victims, and replacing Council Framework Decision 2002/629/JHA.

the performance of his or her duties is now treated as an aggravating issue in sentencing.

Administrative Immigration Arrangements for the Protection of Victims of Trafficking were introduced in June 2008 to coincide with the commencement of the Criminal Law (Human Trafficking) Act 2008. If potential trafficked victims have no legal basis to remain in the State, a 60-day recovery and reflection period and/or a six-month renewable temporary residence permission can be granted, where the person wishes to assist the authorities in any investigation or prosecution relating to alleged trafficking.

Amendments were made in 2011, allowing a victim to apply for longer term permission to remain in Ireland after three years of temporary residence permissions, or when the human trafficking investigation or prosecution is complete. They also allowed for a recovery and reflection period for children of over 60 days, to arrange for their care and welfare. Those refused asylum will be identified as a victim of human trafficking in immigration considerations. It is intended that these arrangements will be given legislative effect in the Immigration, Residence and Protection Bill, currently before the Irish Parliament.

Engagement with key stakeholders

In late 2007 the Minister of Justice and Equality established a *High Level Interdepartmental Group* to recommend the most appropriate and effective response to trafficking in human beings and to oversee the development and implementation of the States National Action Plan. This includes senior representatives from the Departments of Justice and Equality; Health; Children and Youth Affairs; Jobs, Enterprise and Innovation; An Garda Síochána (the Irish police) and the Health Services Executive.

Together we had to agree arrangements which needed to be put in place to give effect to Ireland's international obligations. In the light of general recommendations by the Organization for Security and Co-operation in Europe (OSCE) we decided to establish a *Roundtable* Forum of senior representatives from the key NGOs and international organizations, with whom the High Level Group would engage about 2 or 3 times a year.

The High Level Group approved the establishment of five interdisciplinary Working Groups which I chaired. They include representatives from the relevant government agencies, NGOs and international organizations and their role is to progress matters at a practical, on-the-ground level, in relation to the implementation of the National Action Plan and report on the work being carried out.

Initially each of the groups met about every 3-4 months and I chaired over 80 meetings during my four-year term as Executive Director. The Working Groups deal with development of a National Referral Mechanism (the services for victims), awareness raising and training, child trafficking, labor exploitation and sexual exploitation. Over 70 different governmental, NGOs and international organizations are involved with the Anti-Human Trafficking Unit's activities.

National Action Plan

As soon as the consultative structures were put in place, the AHTU took a twin-track approach. We developed a National Action Plan for the government's approval, while applying initial measures to combat and prevent human trafficking. In view of the economic climate, we sought to balance what could be realistically achieved within available resources, with Ireland's international obligations and our determination to provide the best possible services to victims of trafficking.

The National Action Plan to Prevent and Combat Trafficking in Human Beings for the period 2009-2012 was published by the Minister for Justice and Equality in June 2009[9]. The plan set out a total of 144 measures to prevent human trafficking in Ireland, protect possible and suspected victims and to enforce the relevant

---

9. National Action Plan is available at www.blueblindfold.gov.ie

legislation. It also set out key areas for prevention, protection and prosecution.

Awareness-raising

Ireland took a lead role in the Awareness-Raising Strand of the G6 initiative[10]. A national campaign was launched in late 2008, establishing a dedicated state anti-trafficking website, which used the 'Blue Blindfold' slogan, 'Don't close your eyes to human trafficking'[11]. Similar campaigns were also arranged in the other G6 countries, adapted in terms of language, content and messaging.

Funding was provided to the NGO Ruhama in 2008 for a 3-minute film and a 50-second advertisement designed to educate persons involved or potentially involved in commercial sexual exploitation and the demand side of sex trafficking. The advertisement was aired at the times deemed most appropriate to reach target audiences on the national television station and on a sports television station.

The Department of Education and Science helped us involve teachers and students in raising awareness by including the topic of human trafficking as part of the Human Rights module of the Civil, Social and Political Education course in secondary schools. Resource materials were developed, including the booklet, 'Don't close your eyes to slavery.'

Funding to build capacity in source countries was also provided under the Overseas Development Programme. Awareness-raising seminars for staff in the Department of Foreign Affairs and Trade being posted abroad and staff in the Department of Enterprise and Innovation dealing with work permit applications were also held, and articles included in various professional magazines and newsletters.

---

10. The G6 initiative was an anti-trafficking initiative involving 6 EU countries – Ireland, UK, Poland, Italy, Netherlands and Spain – supported by Interpol, Europol and Eurojust.
11. See website www.blueblindfold.gov.ie for details and information on anti-human trafficking measures.

Training

A key consideration was to advise state employees about human trafficking and what to do if they encountered or suspected it. Awareness-raising training was delivered by the International Organization for Migration, with presentations by the Health Service Executive, NGOs, the Garda (Police) National Immigration Bureau and the AHTU on the indicators of human trafficking.

Personnel from organizations such as the Health Service Executive, National Employment Rights Authority Inspectors, Private Security Authority Inspectors, staff of the Irish Naturalisation and Immigration Service and of the Office of Refugee Applications Commissioner, Victims of Crime Office, Crime Victims Helpline, Probation Service, Youth Detention Schools and staff of the Departments of Jobs, Enterprise and Innovation and Social Protection received this training.

A training course was also developed by An Garda Síochána – which continues to be rolled out – to enable them to identify victims, refer them to appropriate services and initiate criminal investigations. The course is entitled 'Tackling Trafficking in Human Beings: Prevention, Protection and Prosecution.' The International Organization for Migration, the United Nations, the Health Services Executive and NGOs assist in delivering this training to front-line police (including from other forces).

Probationer police also receive training on the identification of possible victims through indicators of human trafficking. Awareness-raising training has also been delivered to Senior Investigating Officers, members of the Garda reserve, ethnic liaison officers and Immigration Officers, as well as for all defense forces personnel on overseas missions.

Specialized training was delivered in 2009 to staff of the Legal Aid Board. The Board established a dedicated unit who provide legal advice to potential and suspected victims. Refresher training took place in 2012.

A data-collection strategy, modeled on systems being developed by the EU, was also put in place to assess the nature and extent of the issue. Information on cases of possible/suspected trafficking is collected by means of a standardized template from key state organizations and NGOs, according to the definition in the Criminal Law (Human Trafficking) Act. Between 1 January 2009 and 31 December 2012 a total of 249 alleged victims of human trafficking were reported to An Garda Síochána[12].

Penalties and policing measures

A range of penalties and policing measures were also put in place, including penalties for carriers operating aircraft, ferries or other vehicles bringing passengers to Ireland without adequate immigration documentation (under the Immigration Act 2003). Penalties also applied for fraud, use and control of false documents including passports and travel documents (under the Criminal Justice [Theft and Fraud] Offences Act 2001).

Training was provided by police for airline staff, and where appropriate, technology was (and is) used to establish if persons were being smuggled into the State concealed in vehicles. Police co-operation with key partners has resulted in successful prosecutions.

Key protection measures

A range of measures were also developed to protect and assist victims of trafficking. Depending on the status and needs of the individual, these include accommodation for potential or suspected adult victims in the Reception and Integration Agency of the Irish Naturalisation and Immigration Service.

The services provided include an individual health care plan developed by a dedicated unit of the Health Services Executive, psychological and material assistance, translation and interpretation,

---

12. See summary statistical reports for each of the years on www.blublindfold.gov.ie

legal aid and advice by the State's Anti-Trafficking Team in the Legal Aid Board, access to the labor market, vocational training and education for those not in the asylum system, and policing services including security advice and witness protection, repatriation or return and compensation. For victims granted temporary residence, dedicated personnel in the New Communities and Asylum Seekers Unit in the Department of Social Protection facilitate the move from Reception and Integration Agency accommodation to independent living.

Victim care is also provided by non-governmental organizations. Victims are informed of the support services provided by organizations, such as Ruhama and Cork Sexual Violence Centre in the area of trafficking for sexual exploitation. Victims of trafficking for labor exploitation are advised of the Migrant Rights Centre services. The Immigrant Council of Ireland also serves victims of trafficking as an independent law center. In addition, two faith-based NGOs – Act to Prevent Trafficking (APT) and Tirzah – work to prevent and to raise awareness of human trafficking.

For child victims, separate accommodation is made available with additional services such as a multidisciplinary assessment of needs before preparing an individual care plan, education and, where appropriate, tracing of family members.

Funding was (and continues to be) provided to Ruhama – a charity assisting victims of sexual exploitation. Funding has since been provided to the Migrants Rights Centre of Ireland who help victims of labor exploitation.

Key Measures for the Prosecution and Investigation of Human Trafficking

When the plan was published, An Garda Síochána had taken a number of proactive measures, including Operation Snow, designed to prevent the trafficking of minors into, out of and within the State, to secure their welfare and ensure prosecutions. A person suspected of trafficking up to 100 children into Europe was arrested in Ireland and surrendered to the Netherlands where he was sentenced to 6 years imprisonment in his absence.

Close co-operation is in place with the United Kingdom. In 2008/ 2009 Ireland participated in a multi-agency operation responding to human trafficking called Operation Pentameter. To prevent and combat offences, close co-operation with international organizations such as Europol, Interpol, Eurojust and Frontex continues.

The 2009 Policing Plan identified trafficking as a key priority for An Garda Síochána, which it remains. A dedicated Human Trafficking Investigation and Co-ordination Unit was established within the Garda National Immigration Bureau (GNIB) in 2009. This acts as a center of excellence for the organization and oversees all investigations with an element of human trafficking, providing advice, guidance and operational support for investigations. Liaison officers were put in place to work with victims and organizations working with victims. A joint protocol was signed between the police and the HSE, setting out their role in relation to children missing from care.

Key measures since publication of the National Action Plan

Work has continued since the publication of the National Action Plan in the areas of prevention, protection and prosecution. Some of the key measures put in place are set out beneath.

Targeted awareness-raising has continued with groups likely to encounter victims in the course of their work. They include public service personnel such as agricultural inspectors, veterinary personnel, prison officers, probation officers, teachers and educational professionals, doctors and healthcare professionals.

We have also engaged with private company groups, including Reception and Integration Agency service providers, hotels and groups such as the Restaurant Association of Ireland and the Licensed Vintners Association, as well as with secondary and tertiary level students. Articles and advertisements continue to be placed in appropriate publications.

In 2009 the International Organization for Migration secured a contract from the Department of Justice and Equality to develop, design and deliver a 'Train the Trainer' Programme. This program was subsequently delivered to personnel in Government agencies likely to encounter victims of human trafficking. For the purpose of the course, participants subsequently delivered such training in their organizations.

A film festival was held to in October 2010 to coincide with EU Anti-Trafficking Day. Two films were shown, followed by a panel discussion, one with a theme of labor exploitation and the other on sexual exploitation. More than 650 people attended both events, with over 250 transition-year and higher level students attending one of the events. The Blue Blindfold Campaign, initially launched in 2008, was re-launched in both the North and South of Ireland in January 2011.

Artwork from a competition for secondary students was used to illustrate a guide to services provided to victims of child trafficking. A cross-border photographic and video competition with a social media element was launched to coincide with the 6th EU Anti-Trafficking day on 18 October 2012. The competition was open to all tertiary students on the island of Ireland.

Police training, investigation and prosecution continue, as do policing operations and international liaison which have resulted in successful prosecutions. They include sentences of 7 and 5 years respectively imposed in Romania, from evidence gathered in Ireland about the trafficking of 28 people to Ireland for the purposes of labor exploitation. In Lithuania sentences of 11 and 6 years were imposed based on information provided by the Irish authorities about money transfers from Ireland for human trafficking offences.

In Wales, sentences of 7, 3.5 and 2 years imprisonment were imposed for human trafficking, prostitution and money laundering offences. A confiscation order of €2.2 million was also imposed. In that instance most of the criminal activity took place in Ireland.

A web-based portal is available on the Garda computer system which provides a step-by-step guide on what to do if the police suspect a person to be a victim of human trafficking.

The Director of Public Prosecutions nominated particular prosecutors to deal with human trafficking cases and issued guidelines about which factors are to be considered in assessing whether to commence or continue with a prosecution. They include a consideration as to whether the public interest is served by a prosecution of a victim of human trafficking who has been compelled to commit offences (e.g. immigration or sexual offences) as a result of being trafficked.

The International Organization for Migration continues to assist with voluntary return programs and reintegration. A statement of roles and responsibilities between state agencies, NGOs and international organizations has been developed.

The services outlined earlier continue to be provided, as does funding to two NGOs. In 2011 the Department also part-funded a photography exhibition entitled 'Not Natasha,' organized by the Immigrant Council of Ireland. The theme was sex trafficking and its effects on the victims involved.

The data collection strategy remains in place to enable an assessment to be made of the nature and extent of this problem.

Key developments in the future

In 2010, following the wide range of measures put in place, Ireland ratified both the United Nations Protocol against Transnational Organised Crime and the Council of Europe Convention on Action against Trafficking in Human Beings.

A structured review of the implementation of the National Action Plan was carried out during 2011. This involved a consultation process with relevant stakeholders[13]. In 2011 the European Union adopted an EU Directive[14] with an implementation date of April 2013. Ireland is fully compliant with the terms of the Directive, as a result of the administrative and legislative arrangements in place.

A number of developments will inform the next National Action Plan, which is currently being developed, including the EU Strategy towards the Eradication of Trafficking in Human Beings 2012-2016 which was published in October 2012. Others include the recommendations in the Report of the OSCE Special Representative and Coordinator for Trafficking in Human Beings arising from her visit to Ireland in January 2012, the Report arising from the Council of Europe Group of Experts on Action against Trafficking (GRETA) evaluation of Ireland[15] and the US Trafficking in Persons Report.

During the Irish Presidency of the European Union from January to June 2013, Ireland worked closely with the European Commission to give effect to Article 4 of the EU Strategy. This Article relates to the provision of information on the rights of victims. This resulted in the publication in April 2013 of a handbook, *The EU rights of victims of trafficking in human beings* which sets out the rights and supports, derived from EU law, that are available to victims. The document sets out for the first time, in a single document, all relevant EU legislation. The Justice and Home Affairs Council of the European Union agreed in June 2013 that Member States should ensure that information in this easily understandable format will be made available to legal practitioners and victims in all Member States.

The AHTU, in partnership with the NGO Ruhama, has recently secured EU funding under a PROGRESS Grant Scheme related to

---

13. See report at www.blueblindfold.gov.ie
14. See footnote 2.
15. The Reports can be viewed at http://www.blueblindfold.gov.ie/website/bbf/ bbfweb.nsf/page/mews-publications-en. GRETA, established by the Council of Europe, is the body responsible for the monitoring implementation of the Council of Europe Convention on Action against Trafficking in Human Beings by the Parties to the Convention.

Violence against Women in the context of Human Trafficking. The two-year project focuses on activities that will promote zero tolerance of human trafficking as a form of violence against women. In particular the project will address awareness among victims and potential victims for men and will develop innovative training and support to frontline actors including the development of a mobile app.

Conclusion

This is but a brief overview of some of the main measures taken by the Irish State, in conjunction with other relevant stakeholders, to address the scourge of human trafficking. The measures that were put in place in Ireland have been commended on a number of occasions – in 2010 by the London School of Tropical Medicine and by Anti-Slavery International; in 2011 by the Director of the United Nations Office on Drugs and Crime and in 2012 by the Director of the US Human Smuggling and Trafficking Centre. In particular, Ireland has been referred to as a leader in combating trafficking in persons and an innovator in victim care.

The approach by An Garda Síochána to dealing with victims has been described as 'enlightened' and the Health Services Care Plan and the direct referral by the police to them is recommended as a model of international best practice. In addition the US Trafficking in Persons Reports assigned Ireland a 'Tier 1' rating in its 2010, 2011 and 2012 reports[16]. While much has been done, there is more that can be achieved. The Irish Government is committed to tackling human trafficking, supporting victims and pursuing traffickers.

---

16. The US Congress, under the 2000 Trafficking Victims Protection Act as amended (TVPA) requires the Secretary of State to submit an annual Report to Congress setting out the extent of efforts by Governments worldwide to reach compliance with the TVPA minimum standards for the elimination of human trafficking. Countries considered as being countries of origin, transit or destination for victims of severe forms of trafficking are included in what is known as the "TIP Report". They are assigned one of 3 tiers. Countries assessed as meeting the 'minimum standards for the elimination of severe forms of trafficking' set out in TVPA are classified as Tier 1. This is the highest rating a country can receive.

Marion Walsh was appointed as the first Executive Director of the Anti-Human Trafficking Unit in the Department of Justice and Equality in February 2008. A career civil servant, Marion has worked in a wide range of posts in the Department of Justice and Equality. She has been Private Secretary to a number of Ministers for Justice. She has also worked in the Human Resources, Garda (police), Criminal Law Reform and International Policy areas of the Department. She was involved in the setting up of the Office of the Refugee Applications Commissioner and is currently serving in the Crime and Security Directorate of the Department and is a member of the Board of the Private Security Authority and sub-Committees of that Board.

Chapter 21
Bringing the Law
to Bear upon Modern Slavery
Baroness Elizabeth Butler-Sloss

I have been a Christian all my life. I was born into a Church of England family and went to church with my mother, and then to an Anglican boarding school. My father became a High Court judge and I followed him and my elder brother into the practice of law as a barrister; in due course I became a judge.

For centuries the law of England and Wales has been based upon the common law, supplemented by statute law passed by Parliament, which now predominates. Both are based upon the Judeo-Christian moral code. Consequently, my Christian upbringing and the training in the law formed the basis of my approach to my former work as a judge.

It is not possible for a judge in civil and family law always to apply the law so as to do justice to the individual as one's conscience would like to achieve! However, a judge must apply the law fairly to all sides and I have seldom found myself making a decision in which the law and my Christian principles diverged. Archbishop Hapgood, then Archbishop of York, once asked me this directly and I have reflected on it ever since.

As a High Court judge I dealt with families and principally with children. Through this, I learnt about the trafficking of teenage girls from Africa through Gatwick Airport, several of whom came through the family court. I retired from my last post in the law as President of the Family Division in 2005 and in 2006 was appointed to the House of Lords as a cross bench (independent) peer. I decided to begin a new career and to attend the House of Lords regularly and join committees and sit on Select Committees.

I am joint chairman with Fiona Mactaggart MP of an all-party parliamentary group of both Houses of Parliament on human trafficking and modern slavery. I was invited to join the group soon after I became a peer by Anthony Steen, then an MP. He retired from Parliament in 2010 and has since devoted himself tirelessly to combating modern slavery. One does not have to be a Christian to do wonderful work in this cause. One area in which our Parliamentary group has been especially active has been in persuading the Government to sign the EU Human Trafficking Directive.

Anthony Steen set up the Human Trafficking Foundation of which I am a trustee. The Foundation does many useful things, and I am particularly involved in two of them. The first is bringing together non-governmental organizations (NGOs) devoted to every aspect of combating human trafficking and modern slavery with members of Parliament.

Over 80 NGOs attend quarterly meetings to talk to and ask questions of MPs and Peers, Ministers, the Crown Prosecution Service and the Police. The Foundation acts as a bridge between NGOs and Parliament and is unique in bringing together those who would not otherwise necessarily listen to each other.

The second is the Foundation's collaboration with several other charities within the EU to discuss how to combat this evil across Europe. The EU Commission financed, together with generous donations, a project to enable MPs across the EU to meet each other. Groups of MPs from seven or eight countries met in Lisbon, Madrid,

Rome, Helsinki, Warsaw and Ljubljana as well as twice in both London and Bucharest.

In each country we met government ministers, chairmen of the relevant parliamentary committees, the prosecution service, the police and local NGOs. A major purpose was to raise awareness of the scale of the problem in each country and across Europe. We discussed detection, prosecution, data collection, victim identification and support and prevention.

As a result of our meetings we were all much better informed and several countries have set up anti-slavery groups within their parliaments. We need to take this initiative further and continue to work as parliamentarians across Europe. There are, of course, other major initiatives including the meetings between the Pope and the Archbishop of Canterbury and conferences initiated by the Pope in the Vatican.

It is however of the greatest importance to involve MPs across Europe to work with their governments and the agencies. One country which is to be congratulated is Romania, which has major problems but has a good record in prosecutions and convictions of traffickers, far better than the United Kingdom.

The all-party Parliamentary group and the Human Trafficking Foundation have been lobbying Government to pass legislation to assist in the prosecution, conviction of traffickers and the identification and support of the victims. To its credit this government has introduced the Modern Slavery Bill, now going through Parliament.

Prior to the introduction of the Bill, Teresa May MP, the Home Secretary, asked Frank Field MP to set up an informal inquiry into trafficking and slavery. The other two members of this informal inquiry were Sir John Randall MP and myself. We invited written and oral evidence and published a report in December last year. Our report was, I believe, influential in the drafting of the Bill. Home

Office officials attended the evidence meetings we held and received all the written evidence while our inquiry was proceeding.

Once the Bill was published early this year, a pre-legislative Select Committee of fourteen members of both Houses, including the Bishop of Chester, was set up with Frank Field as its chairman and I was vice-chairman. We adopted all the evidence from the informal inquiry and its report and accepted further written and oral evidence. Frank Field was a taskmaster and very often we sat two days a week, both morning and afternoon, in order to complete our report to the Home Secretary by Easter.

Our report was bold in that we drafted our own version of the Bill in place of the Government version. The Government Bill, not surprisingly, does not reflect much of what our Select Committee would like to have seen in it but the Government has made substantial changes reflecting many of our concerns.

One important addition to the Bill is the opportunity for a victim to claim a defense where he or she has been compelled to commit an offence. An obvious example is the Vietnamese boy tending cannabis plants, but locked into a building unable to escape. A decision of the Court of Appeal Criminal Division last summer highlighted the plight of these young people.

The Bill also provides for special measures to support victims giving evidence in the trial of their traffickers and guidance on identifying and supporting victims. For the first time, there will also be a Modern Slavery Commissioner.

Another issue which Lord McColl of Dulwich and I have tried to put into other legislation going through the House of Lords is the need for trafficked children to have an advocate to help them through the tortuous process once the child is identified as a victim. After a great deal of lobbying behind the scenes, Lord McColl, also a member of the Select Committee, and I persuaded the Government to set up a pilot project to test child advocates across the country. This is now being rolled out in many local authorities across the country and is reflected in the Bill in the obligation of the

Home Secretary to report to Parliament on the outcome of the pilot project within nine months of its completion.

Side by side with the Bill, a senior Home Office official has investigated the working of the system identifying and recognizing victims of trafficking, the National Referral Mechanism. His report is about to be published and I hope its recommendations for a major overhaul of the process will be accepted. At the same time as the Select Committee was hearing evidence, one of its members, Fiona Mactaggart MP, chaired another useful inquiry into data collection and its inadequacies.

The Bill is not perfect but is a huge step forward. Naturally during its passage through the House of Lords we shall try to improve it, but, even if we do not, we shall have a major piece of legislation on the statute book. There will be the opportunity further to improve it during the next Parliament.

My daughter once told me that my instinct to accept tasks which I have been asked to take on displays a sense of duty which is much less prevalent today. If she is correct, that is a sad reflection upon modern society.

I was taught both at home and at school a sense of responsibility to society and the requirement to accept where that took me. It sounds pompous written down, but it has led me in to accepting requests which by choice I might not have taken. My friendship with Anthony Steen led me in to the work I have done since 2006 in the field of human trafficking and modern slavery and I feel that it is my duty to continue to help in the small way I can for the foreseeable future.

The Rt Hon the Baroness Butler-Sloss GBE was the first female Lord Justice of Appeal and, until 2004, was the highest-ranking female judge in the United Kingdom. She is Joint-Chair of an all-party parliamentary group of both Houses of Parliament on human trafficking and modern slavery.

Chapter 22
Law Enforcement
Can't Deal With This On Its Own
Nick Kinsella

There's an old saying in Ireland, 'If you're lucky enough to be Irish, then you're lucky enough!'

I was fortunate enough to be born in Dublin, Ireland in 1957. My parents and older brother and I lived with my mother's older sister Mai and her husband Nicky (my namesake), in a tiny 'two-up, two-down' rented house near the docks. I wonder now, looking back, how we all fitted in. There was no bathroom until an extension was built in the sixties and the only toilet was in the small back yard. Our only source of heating was a coal fire in the back downstairs room.

It was there as a boy that I was christened into the Catholic Church and went to my first school, St Joseph's. I had my first sweets – 'penny cones' (a sheet of paper twisted into a small cone and filled with sweets) – from the local shop crammed among the rows of terraced houses. I experienced my first hospital stay (for scarlet fever) and had my first ride in a car (a neighbor's Morris Minor).

I can remember playing out in the street as everybody did then, on a go-cart my dad had made for my brother and me out of old wood and pram wheels. All the kids in the area had one and the races seemed like spectacular and important events. We were not rich in terms of material things, but life was, as they say, 'grand'. I was happy.

At some point in time, like millions of other Irish, we left Ireland. My parents took us to England and we became immigrants. The Church, the Irish community, and our extended family always remained constants, though. We lived in many places in London – and elsewhere – as my father moved from job to job constantly trying to improve our lot.

Sometimes he would go for a job to be met by a sign that read 'No blacks, no Irish.' I couldn't understand that and I never forgot it. Nevertheless, my father always found work and over the years we progressed from renting flats over shops to owning our own home. When the time for retirement came, my parents moved home to Ireland and spent their remaining happy years together there. There is no doubt that we were blessed.

With this upbringing it is no surprise that faith, family and friendship, accompanied by a strong desire for fairness, became core values that would shape my life. Policing was a natural choice of career for me, and I saw it as a vocation, my opportunity to help and to put victims first. Many years later, when I first became aware of human trafficking, the 'victim-centered' approach to supporting survivors and investigating their ordeal seemed to be just plain common sense. Like a doctor, the first rule was to do no harm. I didn't see 'protection' in isolation, but as an integrated part of prosecuting offenders, preventing further criminal activity and working in partnership.

First encounters with human trafficking

When I joined the UK police service in 1980 it never crossed my mind that I would be dealing with modern slavery. I first stumbled across human trafficking as a detective superintendent when I took up the post of Director of Intelligence in my home force. This challenging job incorporated, amongst other things, Covert Operations and the diverse units of the Force Intelligence Bureau. Yet it was 'Organized Immigration Crime' – something I had never heard of – that would change my life.

Part of my new role required me to help build a response to the identified crime threats, but I didn't even know what 'Organized Immigration Crime' (OIC) was. Twenty years in the job had given me plenty of experience in dealing with drug trafficking, burglary and violent crime, yet not this. I soon learnt that the term referred to organized criminals involved in human smuggling and human trafficking. But at that time we simply were not sufficiently aware and prepared to deal with it; there was insufficient training, knowledge and dedicated skills. Things had to change, not just in my force but across the country.

To help raise the issue's profile, the government had just created a multi-agency task force under the banner 'Reflex.' Millions of pounds of funding a year were also made available to build a response. Luckily, I knew someone who worked for the Reflex team who was able to provide a briefing that filled in some gaps in my knowledge.

I was successful in a bid for part of that national funding, which allowed me to create a multi-agency unit dedicated to combatting OIC. Some months later a further bid was submitted to establish similar units in two neighboring police forces, so all three units could work together when needed to provide a wider regional response. Within months that team would begin a serious investigation into the sex trafficking of a fifteen-year-old Lithuanian girl. That investigation would ultimately secure the first conviction in the UK for Human Trafficking.

Broadening the scope

Fourteen months after taking up post I was transferred to the National Criminal Intelligence Service (NCIS) as Assistant Director in charge of International Organized Immigration Crime, (IOI), a branch of the International Division.

NCIS' command team was forward thinking and innovative. They delivered what they said they would deliver and gave us the freedom to do the same. My boss, Rob Wainwright, the Director of International Division, had the 'nous' to surround himself with four experienced detective chief superintendents of police. This highly competent man was not only a great boss, but later became the Head of Europol – the Policing Agency of the European Union, (EU).

My fellow assistant directors in the international division, Brian Minihane, Ken Pandolfi and Patrick Spencer were experienced detectives with significant international experience and we all got on. It was an honour to know them and I acknowledge here my thanks for both their help and friendship. I felt comfortable, supported and empowered. At that time it became clear that nearly all the intelligence into my office was related to human smuggling and very little to trafficking. To tackle any problem, you need to understand it and in law enforcement terms this meant, amongst other things, having good intelligence that can allow more targeted deployment of resources. It was clear that we needed to tackle the intelligence gaps around the issue of trafficking.

Operation Pentameter

I had always seen advantages in pro-active operations and in 2004, to help address the shortfall in knowledge around trafficking, suggested to Rob that every police force in the UK (43 in England and Wales plus the Scottish forces), concentrate some operational resource on one subject – human trafficking – for a set time. Such an operation would be expensive and resource-intensive, but could be invaluable in numerous ways. After asking some insightful questions, Rob gave me his approval and support.

Reflex funded that plan which became 'Operation Pentameter.' It was a huge multi-agency operation led by a chief constable of police but working with numerous statutory and voluntary organizations. Over 80 victims of trafficking were recovered in a three-month period, giving us the first real evidence that trafficking really was a problem in the UK. Intelligence about trafficking rose to new levels and the press coverage was truly international.

The stories of the trauma and exploitation that the victims had been subjected to were horrendous; the youngest victim was just fourteen. Having lifted the stone and discovered the problem, UK law enforcement then had a legal duty of care to do something about it. The problem could not be ignored.

Pentameter was a success, victims were recovered, partnership working was enhanced and intelligence reports increased significantly. However, when the operation stopped, so did the increased intelligence flows on trafficking. It was like turning a tap off. We had raised the profile of the issue and more people were now engaged in the anti-trafficking agenda, but it wasn't being investigated any more on the scale that we would have liked to see. Within the law enforcement arena, more dedicated police units were now in place (I had co-sponsored the creation of the Metropolitan Police unit, for example, again funded by Reflex), but anti-trafficking work was still not embedded across every force as 'core police business.'

Several years on from Pentameter, global reports still reflect the need for enhanced training, more investigations and prosecutions. The UNODC Global Report on Trafficking in Persons 2012 states that a worrying aspect in the response to countering human trafficking remains the low conviction rates, on the level of rare crimes such as homicides in Iceland or kidnappings in Norway. The police cannot tackle this alone, but still need to work harder at detecting and punishing this type of crime.

The United Kingdom Human Trafficking Centre

Not long after Pentameter NCIS was amalgamated into a new agency, the Serious Organized Crime Agency (SOCA). I left NCIS and, supported by the operational commander of Pentameter, planned to create a hub to combat Human Trafficking. In October 2006 the United Kingdom Human Trafficking Centre, (UKHTC), opened for business.

The UKHTC was the first center of its type. It quickly expanded, with staff from various agencies including SOCA, the Crown Prosecution Service, police, Her Majesty's Revenue and Customs, the third sector and the Immigration service. We quickly established local, national and international links, becoming a recognized center of excellence on the subject. The center was the primary link with Europol (the policing agency of the EU), chaired the Interpol human trafficking group and was represented on the new EU group of experts.

The center's plan was based on the 4P's approach of Prevention, Protection, Prosecution and Partnership. We were helped immensely by several organizations, particularly in the support of victims. We could always rely on the Salvation Army, City Hearts and the Madaile Trust to help at short notice.

Over the next four years the center was at the forefront of many things, including raising awareness of human trafficking to law enforcement, key public sector workers, the general public and victims. We ran training courses for senior investigating officers and cascaded training electronically to other police.

Our prevention work created the 'Blue Blindfold' Campaign that became the UK and Irish national campaigns with the strap line, 'It's happening here' and led in part to the UN 'Blue Heart' and US

Blue campaigns. Crimestoppers in Canada also worked with the government there to establish 'Blue Blindfold.'

Whilst the center did not conduct its own investigations, to improve both the number and quality of investigations we established a small team of 'tactical advisors', all experienced detectives with a knowledge of human trafficking. These officers would go wherever they were needed across the country to offer assistance and support in investigations.

A local crime

The center was also at the forefront of work to identify new forms of trafficking. These included the trafficking of young UK girls for sexual exploitation and of UK males for forced labor. These developments were sometimes met with unexpected responses but, sadly, the passage of time has provided ample evidence that these forms of exploitation exist. We began to spread the word that you didn't have to be foreign to be trafficked and that this was very much a local crime impacting our communities. Trafficking in the UK had always been seen within the context of immigration, but we found evidence that UK nationals were also victims. In truth, trafficking is first and foremost a crime and an attack on the victims' fundamental human rights.

The UN Global Trafficking in Persons Report 2012 makes the case for domestic trafficking. It states that most victims detected around the world were foreign nationals in their country of exploitation, but one in four victims detected between 2007 and 2010 was a national of the country where he or she was exploited. During the reporting period, more than 25% of detected victims were trafficked within their country of origin and domestic trafficking had been reported in more than 60 of the 83 countries worldwide that reported information on the nationality of the victims. Domestic trafficking appeared to be increasing year by year in the light of the information collected during the reporting period. In the latest UN GLOBAL Report, published in November 2014, domestic trafficking victims are now reported to account for 34% of the total number of detected victims.

Since official figures began to be collected in the UK in the National Referral Mechanism, UK nationals have consistently been in the top ten nationalities of referred potential victims.

Pentameter 2

In 2007/08 I gained support for another national multi-agency operation, Pentameter 2. Again it was led by a chief constable, and this time over a hundred and fifty potential victims were recovered. An inspired, intelligent and hardworking official at the Home Office was very supportive and helped drive the government agenda forward. She had also built a good team to support her.

The Government soon created the first National Action Plan to combat Human Trafficking and the UK also ratified the Council of Europe Convention. Like other partners, the UKHTC had a growing number of key responsibilities and actions. The Minister in charge of the portfolio was very engaged and motivated. In my opinion things were now moving at pace and real progress was being made. Trafficking as an issue though still hadn't become embedded across the Police service and other areas, and much more still had to be done to raise the public's awareness and provide training.

We still had to create a hostile environment for traffickers and turn trafficking from a low-risk, high-profit crime to a crime that carried a huge risk and small profit. This was a criminal business estimated to make thirty two billion dollars a year through trading in human misery. We had to hit it where it hurt.

In such a situation I believe that people who understand and drive the agenda are crucially important – as seen by examples in this book. Of course, it's not just about individuals – anti-trafficking work needs to be fully integrated in a broad strategic response such as the National Action Plan, but we had been blessed with an outstanding official at the home office who had the respect of all parties. When she left, followed closely by the minister, it was, in my opinion, a double blow.

Within twelve months the decision had been taken to move the UKHTC into SOCA. The center had been initially established within the policing environment under the oversight of a multi-agency group chaired by a chief constable. This had initially worked well but as the center's role developed, (for example, carrying out non-traditional policing functions such as formally identifying victims under the National Referral Mechanism), this structure became less appropriate. Some of us would have liked to see the center obtain its own legal entity as an independent body tasked with building and reporting on the national response to trafficking. This could have provided the flexibility to restructure and reform, something hampered by the legitimate restrictions of the policing legal framework.

Unfortunately, there was insufficient support for this concept at the time and the center was moved to another city, losing the majority of its staff including the entire management team.

Carrying the message

I left the police service after thirty years, but have maintained my interest and involvement in combatting slavery. Today in the UK some key messages remain the same – that trafficking is a local crime as well as an international one, and UK nationals male and female are at risk.

Affecting any family

Ironically, those words would prove to be true in the cruelest way when in July 2013 my adult son, who has moderate learning difficulties, was recovered by local police having been exploited for several weeks. In addition to his suffering and the impact on our family, on reflection three points were reinforced in my mind as being important considerations in building a response to modern slavery.

- First, as in many cases, my son was recovered by a front-line officer – reinforcing the importance of training and awareness of the issue to all front-line professionals, not just police but anyone who may come into contact with victims.

- Second, it reinforced the message that this crime is very much a local one and can impact on any family. Some people still believe that trafficking is only about sex, prostitutes and immigrants.

- Third, privacy of the victim is vital. My son's identity was released which stirred a huge amount of media interest that caused him (and us) some distress as he became known as the 'Sheffield Slave.' Is identifying the victim an effective way to protect the victim?

Training front-line professionals

Training of front line professionals has always been a key issue that I, amongst numerous others, have actively promoted. The US Trafficking in Persons Report 2013 recognizes the crucial need for effective training of law enforcement, advocating:

> The importance of an effective law enforcement response in playing a critical role in accurately identifying victims, because human trafficking is first and foremost a crime and therefore law enforcement agencies will lead most trafficking interventions.

The report goes on to state that victim identification efforts are enhanced through the support of high ranking officers, protocols, and targeted training, and that law enforcement officers are also better able to identify victims when they adopt proactive methods to detect and investigate trafficking. It continues:

Specialized anti trafficking units have proven effective because they allow investigators to receive and apply in-depth training, and to learn from experience with multiple cases. Specialized units are most effective when they have broad authority to investigate trafficking cases. E.g. trafficking units located within vice units are limited to or focused primarily on, vice crimes and, while they may be able to identify sex trafficking cases, are unlikely to find cases of forced labor.

While specialized units are important, anti-trafficking responsibilities cannot be limited to a single unit's jurisdiction alone. Human trafficking victims and offenders are more likely to come in contact with local, non-specialized officers, so it is important for such front line officers and their supervisors to be able to recognize trafficking crimes and understand the basics of responding.

Continuous targeted training on the characteristics of a crime improves police officers' ability to recognize and report the crime; conversely inadequate training cripples law enforcement efforts and timely and accurate victim identification.

Ireland's lead

This brings me back to Ireland, the country of my birth. An Garda Siochana, the Irish Police service, have for many years had an established anti-trafficking training program integrated into a strategic plan to tackle human trafficking.

It addresses all the points highlighted in the above report thanks in no small part to the experienced team within the Garda National Immigration Bureau (GNIB), of Detective Inspector Paul Malloy and Detective Sergeant Claire McKeon, and led by Detective Chief Superintendent John O'Driscoll. In many ways, in my opinion, Ireland is leading the way in embedding training on the issue.

During the years that I have been involved in anti-trafficking work I have met many people from a variety of backgrounds, including politicians, government officials, law enforcement agencies, charities, NGOs and journalists, to list just a few. Some, like those who have contributed to this book, came from a background of faith, but others had no faith. I found one or two to be truly inspirational. Most were good, honest and dedicated people doing the best they could in a difficult area.

One or two I found difficult to work with and for any error or offence caused on my part I apologize. Working in the field of combatting modern slavery can be challenging, stressful and difficult, but it is occasionally – particularly when victims are successfully recovered – immensely rewarding. The key, of course, is preventing people becoming victims in the first place.

* * * * *

I hope that those of you who have been interested enough to read this book find inspiration from the people who have contributed to it and feel compelled to become involved in responsible anti-trafficking work or to support those who are. There is certainly plenty to do.

There are now estimated to be as many as twenty-one million people held in some form of modern slavery, more than at any other time in history. This is truly shocking, but while the situations continue to exist that force ordinary people like you and me to take risks to improve our lives, it will continue to be a problem.

Modern slavery offences are some of the most serious problems facing our globalized society. Some 200 years after the abolition of slavery in the British Empire and similar moves worldwide, modern day slavery exists in many forms, perhaps the most prominent and well defined being human trafficking. All nations and their citizens are affected by the consequences of this form of human rights abuse.

Slavery is now accepted as the second most profitable form of global organized crime. In 2007, the International Labor Organization estimated that the Trafficking Industry generated 32 Billion US Dollars, more than Nike, Google and Starbucks combined. Despite the global recession, Forced Labor in the Private Economy is now estimated to generate $150 Billion', 99 Billion from Commercial Sexual Exploitation and 51 Billion from forced economic exploitation; (including Domestic work, agriculture and other economic activities). (Profits and Poverty; The Economics of Forced Labor – ILO – 2014).

The challenges posed by human trafficking and other forms of modern slavery are immense. This global phenomenon affects States, cities and local communities. Whilst it is a largely hidden problem, it occurs on the streets of our towns and cities where people are trafficked and exploited for sexual and labor purposes. It is present in all our communities with victims coming from all countries, including from within the UK.

Whilst there are many underlying causes for slavery, including globalisation, family breakdown, gender discrimination, weak laws, increased demand, wars, natural disaster and political instability; a key issue in the slavery debate is the cycle of poverty and inequality.

Education can play an important role in breaking that cycle. Awareness raising, training and education campaigns are vital tools in defeating slavery.

No agency or government can deal with this problem alone. There needs to be a broad multi-agency and multi-governmental response that not only tackles the consequences of human exploitation but also addresses the underlying causes. Much is being done but there is still much more to do. Individuals from all walks of life can help combat this crime. Independent action should not be taken. Such action can put yourself and others at risk, but established anti slavery organizations are always seeking help.

I heard a phrase once that captured why we should become involved: "At the very worst time in their lives, the very least that we can do is our very best." Can you help?

Nick Kinsella has been involved in combatting human trafficking for many years and is an acknowledged expert in the field internationally. He held a number of senior positions within both the UK Police service, the National Criminal Intelligence Service (NCIS) and Her Majesty's Inspectorate of Constabulary (HMIC). Nick has played a key role in the development of the UK anti-trafficking strategy and is regarded as one of its founding architects. He created the multi-agency teams that secured the first UK conviction for Human Trafficking and is also responsible for the two largest and most successful national anti-trafficking operations and campaigns in the UK. In 2006 he founded the United Kingdom Human Trafficking Centre, (UKHTC), serving as Chief Executive Officer. In 2008 he founded the UK fund for Victims of Human Trafficking. Nick holds a First Class Degree in Law, and is a qualified teacher. He was awarded the Queens Police Medal, (QPM), in the 2009 UK New Year's Honours List. Nick was a board member for the United Nations Global Trust Fund for victims of Trafficking 2010–2013.

The Delphi Indicators of Trafficking in Human Beings

(entire document can be downloaded from: http://www.truthuncovered.eu)

The Delphi Methodology was developed in the 1950s as a means of producing a result from data gathered from a wide group of experts. This methodology was used to reach a consensus on the indicators that show human trafficking is taking place. Experts were selected from the 27 EU Member States from police, government, academic and research institutes, NGOs, international organizations, labor inspectorates, trade unions and judiciaries.

The results showed four sets of operational indicator categories for adult and child victims of trafficking for labor and sexual exploitation. Each set contains the following types of indicators:

- Deceptive recruitment (or deception during recruitment, transfer and transportation)
- Coercive recruitment (or coercion during recruitment, transfer and transportation)
- Recruitment by abuse of vulnerability
- Exploitative conditions of work
- Coercion at destination
- Abuse of vulnerability at destination

Within each category are *strong*, *medium* and *weak* indicators of trafficking. Space doesn't allow for the full reproduction of all the indicators in each of the categories – and the authors encourage readers to download the full PDF for themselves from *http://www.truthuncovered.eu* – but, listed below are some of the common indicators from each category:

Trafficking of Adults for Labor Exploitation

- Deceived about nature of the job, location or employer
- Violence on victims
- Abuse of illegal status
- Excessive working days or hours
- Bad living conditions
- Confiscation of documents
- Debt bondage
- Isolation, confinement or surveillance
- Forced tasks or clients
- Dependency on exploiters

Trafficking of Adults for Sexual Exploitation

- Deceived about the nature of the job or location
- Deceived about conditions of prostitution
- Abduction, forced marriage, forced adoption or selling of victim
- Threats of violence against victim
- Threat of denunciation to authorities
- Abuse of difficult family situation
- Abuse of lack of information
- No social protection (contract, social insurance etc.)
- Forced into illicit/criminal activities
- Withholding of wages

Trafficking of Children for Labor Exploitation

- Deceived about access to education opportunities
- Deceived about conditions of work
- Deceived about family reunification
- Deceived about wages/earnings
- Threats to inform family, community or public
- Abuse of cultural/religious beliefs
- Excessive working days or hours
- Hazardous work
- Threats of violence against victim
- Violence on family (threats or effective)
- Trafficking of Children for Sexual Exploitation

Deceived about conditions of prostitution

- Deceived about housing and living conditions
- Violence on victims
- Abuse of difficult family situation
- Abuse of lack of education (language)
- Control of exploiters
- Forced tasks or clients
- Isolation, confinement or surveillance
- Forced to lie to authorities, family etc.
- Withholding of wages